CANADIAN RETIREMENT PLANNING MISTAKES

KEY STRATEGIES ON HOW TO TAKE ACTION TO AVOID THEM

GRANT W. HICKS
RDB, CIM, FCSI
FELLOW OF THE CANADIAN SECURITIES
INSTITUTE AND RETIREMENT PLANNING
SPECIALIST

Bright Ideas for Your Retirement Lifestyle

ook online at www.trafford.com
ers@trafford.com

d titles are also available at major online book retailers.

Ronan Lannuzel–Made By Design
.G. LandelsOther Books by Grant W. Hicks

rketing For Financial Advisors
cks and Jay Conrad Levinson
lishing September 2003

rketing on the Front Lines (contributing author)
es Publishing August 2008

rarians: A cataloguing record for this book is available from Library
Canada at www.collectionscanada.ca/amicus/index-e.html

ictoria, BC, Canada.

-4269-1354-9 (sc)

is to efficiently provide the world's finest, most comprehensive
ing service, enabling every author to experience success.
ow to publish your book, your way, and have it available
isit us online at www.trafford.com

02/17/2010

afford. www.trafford.com
LISHING
rica & international

This book covers strategies in four areas for financial security in retirement:

Simplify–Simplify your finances.
Manage–Build a retirement income plan and an investment strategy.
Reduce–Minimize and defer taxes.
Protect–Protect your assets.

IMPORTANT MESSAGES PLEASE READ

IMPORTANT DISCLAIMER PLEASE READ

Grant W. Hicks, RDB, C.I.M., FCSI, Retirement Planning Specialist with Hicks Financial Inc. The views and opinions contained in this book are those of Grant W. Hicks. Information provided is not a solicitation and although obtained from sources considered reliable, is not guaranteed. All names are fictitious and a product of the authors' imagination. All tax-related information is subject to change and is considered reliable, but it is not guaranteed and will change. Always consult your tax and legal professional for verification of any information provided. The author and publisher expressly disclaim any liability, loss, or risk, personal or otherwise, incurred as a direct or indirect consequence of the use or application of the contents of this book.

For comments or questions, Grant can be reached by phone at 250-954-0247 or 866-954-0247, by email at grant@ghicks.com, or on the Web at www.ghicks.com.

Partial proceeds from the sale of this book will be donated by Grant Hicks to :

Nanaimo and District Hospital Foundation.
For more information go to www.nanaimohospitalfoundation.com

NANAIMO & DISTRICT

HOSPITAL
FOUNDATION

Funding Healthcare Needs

Central Vancouver Island

DEDICATIONS

To my wife, Kim, for her creative genius, brilliant ideas, boundless energy, humor, and wit. Thanks for putting up with me and helping me with the struggle of writing.

To Madison and Austin, for their love and support and encouraging me to play instead of work.

The greatest gift a person could receive, an awesome wife and two awesome children with whom to share my life.

ACKNOWLEDGEMENTS

My wife, Kim, who supports me 100% and without whom I could not have completed this book.

My clients, who listen and understand my passion in the financial industry and who place in me their trust and confidence to manage their financial goals and dreams.

My most valuable team, Kim Hicks, Tracy Levirs, and Susan Atchison, who support me with their excellent work, their positive attitudes, and their support.

My valuable clients—with special thanks to my top clients and friends, Bob and Sheila Smith, for their help at seminars, for referrals, and for their genuine business support.

My parents for having confidence in me and supporting my ambitions.

The investment companies for their support and education.

Jay Conrad Levinson, who showed me a few words can have enormous impact on people for years to come.

Finally, a big thanks to you, the reader, who is like me and wants to learn more about retirement and enjoying a great lifestyle for years to come.

TABLE OF CONTENTS

INTRODUCTION

This book is written for retirees who want to learn more, to think differently, and to enhance their retirement lifestyles. It has been a dream since I entered the financial business in 1989 and comes out of years of notes collected at seminars, trade shows, courses, meetings, and conferences. In listening and in writing the notes, I had one goal in mind–to educate retirees about what I have learned and experienced over the years.

A number of common mistakes and problems appeared over and over. Mistakes costly in money, time, and energy. Mistakes that can be avoided by making some simple financial adjustments. You see, I have not retired, far from it; but in doing the job of dealing with retirement day in and day out, I have learned.

With so many Canadians planning to retire or already retired, it might seem easier to plan for retirement in the traditional way; but as time goes on, one might realize there are different ways to think about retirement. Albert Einstein once said, "The significant problems we face cannot be solved by the same level of thinking that created them." So how do we change our level of thinking?

We need a paradigm shift, or a different way of looking at retirement. Not until we start to think outside the box can we discover what the other options are. The human mind is like a parachute–it only works when it is open. So open the book and open your mind to thinking about possibilities and what else you can you do to enhance your lifestyle during retirement.

Retirement planning specialists like me are constantly bombarded by ideas from investment literature, conferences, colleagues, managers, industry publications, wholesalers, and head office. We collect the information and put it to use. Then next week, month, year, we hear about another great idea and make changes to our business. At the end of five years in this business we come to realize that nothing is new, there are just different spins on old ideas. I want to dispel some new ideas and give you tried-and-true concepts, proven over time.

Most retirees are after four things. First and foremost, they want to achieve and maintain financial security. Second, they want to simplify their finances and get rid of "hassle assets" such as real estate or holding companies. Third, they have the time to pay attention to taxes and want to minimize their tax bite each year in retirement. Finally, they want to protect their assets.

Explore the ideas in this book. Learn from an advisor who has helped hundreds of retirees since 1989. Then take those ideas and your thoughts to your accountant, lawyer, financial professional, and team of professional advisors to get the advice you deserve. Start today by making a to-do list. Speak to your financial professionals before proceeding on any idea. Only then will you start to enjoy your fruits of your success.

Dear Reader,

While in Maui at an investment conference, I was lying on the beach thinking about how I could help retirees avoid common and sometimes costly financial mistakes. Sitting under the scorching hot sun and looking out at the aqua-blue water made me think and ask a deep question–what is my purpose in life? Is it to retire? Then it hit me like a ton of bricks. My purpose is to help others retire and create a comfortable lifestyle.

I took out a pad of paper and created *The Island Lifestyle Retirement and Estate Planning Program*©. A system, as it were, gleaned from working with and studying successful retirees for a decade. Success leaves clues, and the pattern emerging from these people is exactly the one I want to follow for my own retirement–a pattern of fundamentals and values for living in retirement. At the opposite end of the spectrum a very clear pattern of opposites or mistakes began to emerge. I could spot them a mile away. Navigating those dangers is like cycling through a row of cactus plants. Stray a little off course and the needles will bite into you.

The people that were "on course" were easy to manage and work with. People that had been off course were tougher in their definition of "comfortable retirement." Until I showed them the prickly cactuses that were in their paths, they were not clear how to navigate.

Let me give you a more personal example. Investing my own money in the 1990s, I was heavily invested into aggressive stocks, as conventional wisdom dictates. I was in my thirties, I had a long time horizon, and I had a high tolerance for risk. Some years I would make a lot of money and would invest in equity funds on the stock market. However, my "comfortable" retirement clients made money, drew some income, and compounded their wealth. I decided to invest in a similar way. My investments became, and continue to be, more conservative; they return more consistently year after year, compounding my wealth. I don't really need to change my risk tolerance in my retirement, since it is already invested that way.

This book is about leaving you with the clues for your own success. I will show you how to steer clear of pitfalls and costly mistakes. Only you and your family know what "comfortable retirement" means to you. Your values towards money never change. This book will help you work towards your values and give you a framework to build that comfortable retirement. It will show you strategies for really stretching your retirement income dollar, for paying less tax, and for having peace of mind with your estate.

Go for it and good luck.

Sincerely,
Grant W. Hicks, CIM, FCSI

P.S. This is not a recommendation for any product or service. Always consult with your accountant, lawyer, financial professional, and team of professional advisors before proceeding on any idea in this book. It is up to you to get professional advice before making any decision about your retirement.

Chapter 1

SIMPLIFY

BUILDING A BETTER RETIREMENT INCOME PLAN FOR A BETTER RETIREMENT LIFESTYLE

GRANT HICKS

What lies behind you and what lies ahead of you pales in comparison with what lies within you.
Ralph Waldo Emerson

Mistake 1
NO CLEAR WRITTEN RETIREMENT PLAN; NOT TAKING CONTROL OF YOUR FINANCIAL FUTURE

The road to financial freedom, wealth, and prosperity requires an accurate map that will let you plot a journey, monitor progress, and change direction if you venture off course. To help you get there, here are ten ideas for developing a sound financial plan with your financial professional.

1. Know where you stand–complete a net worth statement listing assets and liabilities.

2. Define your financial goals based on personal needs and wants.

3. Know how much money you need now, five and ten years from now, and in retirement–including inflation and taxes. Consider increasing your net income by reducing or deferring taxes.

4. Increase discretionary savings by decreasing your expenses.

5. Know your monthly cash flow needs and separate that from major annual expenses such as trips, cars, home renovations, etc.

6. Expand your knowledge of financial issues and economics–check out the library.

7. Reduce or defer income taxes wherever possible. Review your tax plans and make sure your financial advisor has a copy of your tax return.

8. Develop a sound plan for your estate including wills, powers of attorney, and life insurance–lower monthly life insurance costs can save you money.

9. Adjust plans and goals as your circumstances change and review your written plans at least once a year to track your progress.

10. Use the services of professionals (accountant, financial advisor, lawyer). These professionals usually pride themselves on keeping their clients up to date when taxes, investments, and laws change.

If you are not retired now, how much do you need to retire? We all want to retire someday. Some may be wishing it was sooner than later. Here are some ideas to help you.

First, retire to an income, not an age. How much income do you need to live on? Think in terms of monthly income. Once you have an idea of how much you need to live on per month, think of a large emergency or slush fund to spend in early retirement. For example, this money can be spent on large items, outside your monthly budget, such as extended vacations, home renovations, or vehicles.

Second, plan for where the money will come from. Factor in when pensions will kick in (for example; company pension(s), Canada Pension, and old age pensions). You can usually find this with your notice from the Canada Pension Plan statement mailed to you or you can request a copy to be mailed to you: <http://www.servicecanada.gc.ca/en/online/soc/proceed.shtml>. Then add up all of your investments, such as stocks, bonds, GICs, mutual funds, and RRSPs. Take the total amount and expect income to generate from 4% to 6% annually; however, this depends on your risk tolerance, time horizon, and how long you want the money to last. Take an average of 5%, for example, of $200,000, which will generate additional income of $10,000 per year or $833 per month. Finally, look at real estate and businesses. Do you plan to sell off real estate and downsize or generate income from rental real estate? Do you plan to sell any businesses or generate income from them? Now that you have all the sources of capital, ask yourself what percentage of capital you would like to have at the age of 85. Do you want 100% of your money, 50% of your money, or do you want it all spent by then? This will help determine your time horizon as well as your estate wishes. Remember to retire to an income and lifestyle, not an age.

You'll go out on a limb sometimes because that is where the fruit is.
Will Rogers

Early to bed early to rise, work like heck and advertise.
Ted Turner

Mistake 2

NOT SEEING DANGER SIGNS IN YOUR PORTFOLIO

Problem: Unless you're an asset-allocation specialist, how do you know whether your portfolio is matched to your risk tolerance?

Here's a fact for you. In a study by Brinson, Singer, and Beebower (1991) *Financial Analysts Journal*, asset allocation accounts for 91% of portfolio performance, with security selection and market timing factors accounting for less than 5%. Knowing this fact, most investors focus on specific securities or market timing on which to base investment decisions, yet this accounts for less than 10% of the performance. Stop wasting your time. Think about making use of asset allocation strategies to improve your performance. When an investor is frustrated with lack of performance, nine times out of ten it is based on asset allocation and a lack of diversification.

One danger sign common to most portfolios is lack of structure. To build a successful portfolio you need to have multiple asset classes (stocks, bonds, cash, alternative strategies, real estate); multiple styles (value, growth, income, and small, medium, and large capitalization); multiple geographic components (Canada, US, Europe, Asia); and multiple income components (interest-sensitive equities, Government bonds, Corporate bonds, real return bonds, high-yield bonds, mortgages, international bonds, term deposits). Let's face it, diversification is not just buying a few stocks and a few bonds. Here are the remaining nine danger signs possibly lurking in your portfolio.

1. Lack of clear investment policy statement (IPS)—a structure that is clearly defined and understood. Ask your financial advisor for your IPS for your portfolio.

2. Investments mismatched with objectives or risk tolerance—understanding risk and how it relates to your money and portfolio.

3. Under-performing investments or managers—know when to hold them and know when to fold them.

4. Style drift portfolios—that look at risk-adjusted return.

5. Overlapping investments or management styles.

6. Excessive expenses or trading activity.

7. Lack of a system or lack of regular monitoring, adjusting, and rebalancing.

8. Unclear or untimely reporting—when do you review this stuff?

9. Lack of communication and service.

Speak to your financial advisor today about potential danger signs in your portfolio. These danger signs will be discussed in more detail in this book.

Success comes to those who set goals and pursue them regardless of obstacles and disappointments.
Napoleon Hill

The future depends on what we do in the present.
Mahatma Ghandi

Mistake 3
FOUR MAJOR PITFALLS OF RETIREMENT

Most retirees have a plan. Miss one of the four key numbers in your calculations, and you could be headed for disaster.

Investing in retirement can be tricky, as it requires that you consider several factors of lesser concern to younger investors. Make a mistake and you could find yourself surviving on less income than you planned, paying more in taxes, or leaving a smaller legacy to your heirs.

1. Planning for the right time horizon. Longevity is the #1 risk facing retirees. Your life expectancy, if you are now 65, is at least 20 years more; but that represents an average. Many seniors live much longer. In fact, a 65-year-old male has a 25% chance of living past 92; a female has a 25% chance of living past 94. Thus that 20-year number isn't very useful when it comes to individual planning.

2. Market Risks. Retirees still need to invest a portion of their nest egg for growth yet cannot afford to take on the same level of risk as a younger person, because there is less time to make up for bad decisions.

3. Inflation. Most investors do not realize that your income must double every twenty years just to keep up with the average rate of inflation. Many pensions do not include a cost-of-living adjustment; thus your personal savings will have to either grow adequately to cover inflation, or be large enough to allow you to draw an ever-increasing amount of income.

4. Starting retirement with too large a draw-down. The amount of income you need to draw from your savings to maintain your lifestyle will increase with time. Other costs, such as medical

expenses, will likely also rise as you grow older. Most retirees will need to start somewhere in the 3% to 6% range, then allow increases to that amount for inflation. Figuring out what you should take will require analysis of your life expectancy, the number of guaranteed lifetime income sources you have (such as pensions or annuities), and the composition of your portfolio.

In conclusion, when it comes to developing your financial plan for your retirement, you need to pay close attention to details that were less important when you were younger. Fortunately, it is possible to structure most portfolios to protect yourself from running out of money. Your best defense is to address your specific needs, concerns and desires, and ask for help from your financial institution or financial professional to develop a plan and portfolio that will allow you to sleep comfortably in the knowledge that your life will remain financially secure.

We are or become those things which we repeatedly do. Therefore, excellence can become not just an event but a habit.
Albert Einstein

You must be the change you wish to see in the world.
Mahatma Ghandi

Mistake 4
SIMPLE MONEY MISTAKES ANY RETIREE CAN AVOID

Every day newspapers carry headlines that worry retirees. The challenge is learning about the risks. While the world is changing and the markets evolve over time, learning and understanding risk and the obstacles can be a challenge. Here are some simplified ideas.

The difference between having and not having money is simple. The wealthy invest their money first and spend what is left. The people without a great deal of money spend what they have and try to save what is left. Do you have an automatic saving or investing program, or are you waiting until all your bills are paid?

What other mistakes do people make with money?

Investing without purpose. Do you just want more money, to travel more, to go to Hawaii in the winter, or to go skiing with your family?

Do you have an investment rebalancing program? Do you just invest and hope that it rides out the poor periods and grows rapidly in the good times, or do you and your portfolio manager(s) have a system for rebalancing in good times and bad for optimum interest rates? Have you ever invested in a GIC or locked into a mortgage for five years only to soon find you could have saved or gained another half to one percentage point? You shop around for the best prices in groceries and clothing, why not do the same with your investments?

Not understanding risk—perhaps the greatest mistake of the last decade. When stock markets sank and real estate skyrocketed, did you feel comfortable with your overall diversification plan? Or was it all in stocks, and forced you to learn about risk and diversification the hard way? Do you have a diversified portfolio or just a couple of big bets?

Currency risks. Hey, who knew the Canadian dollar would rise dramatically against the US dollar? Going global is great, but it is worth diversifying to avoid wiping out your gains by speculating which way the Canadian dollar will go.

Do you only dream of retirement income, or do you invest so you will have a predictable and comfortable retirement income? Knowing this can be the difference between having money or not in your retirement.

Anyone who has never made a mistake has never tried anything new.
Albert Einstein

If you don't know where you are going, you'll end up some place else.
Yogi Berra

Mistake 5
NOT MANAGING MONEY SYSTEMATICALLY

The new buzzword in the investment industry is "program." It seems several well-known investment companies have developed their own programs. Each company has unique names and features for its programs. Examining the differences of programs can be as confusing as picking next year's hot fund. What you need to find out is whether these investment plans are suitable for you.

Of what benefit is it to go into a plan or program with your money? There are several concerns you should have when looking at investing into these types of investment plans; but first let me explain that these are processes of managing money, not specific investments. If you want to invest into a mutual fund, the process is to examine your risk and determine your needs, such as growth or income, then choose suitable investments.

The newest way to invest is into company programs. The process can be as simple as picking a particular portfolio, or it can be tailored to your specific needs (such as tax minimization, income planning, capital preservation, or a combination of needs.) While the industry looks to gain back the confidence of investors, programs vary dramatically in costs, rebalancing, sophistication, and true benefits to you, the investor. Be careful not to just buy into a program without asking some key questions like: How does this program stack up against other programs? What types of reports will I receive? How does it measure up against benchmarks such as indexes or GICs? Who is involved in the process? How do they accommodate my specific investment needs? What are the minimums to invest? (Some companies have minimums of $25,000 to $250,000 or more.) Finally, be aware that there are several programs available in Canada today, and a one-size-fits-all solution may not accommodate your changing lifestyle or investment needs. Maybe you need two programs to make the right fit or the appropriate diversification. Examine what is important to you about money; then find out whether a program, or two, is right for you. Remember to manage your money like a system, or hire people who have a system that inspires in you confidence that your money will work as hard for you as you do for it.

Meeting Your Needs Through Diversification

Every day I am asked the same question: "Grant, why do I need to be more diversified?" I usually respond along the following lines.

Because my crystal ball is broken and I do not know what the future holds. I did not predict oil and gas going from $10 to $140 a barrel, and I sure did not predict that the Government would announce a tax on income trusts. However, this is what I know for sure. Highly diversified portfolios tend to have less volatility and less dramatic ups and downs than nondiversified portfolios. They contain as many as fifteen asset classes and are managed like pension plans, but unlike pension plans, managed asset programs are designed to match your specific goals and objectives, allowing for dynamic security selection, regular rebalancing reviews, comprehensive tax record-keeping, and client-friendly, easy-to-understand information. The process is very detailed but easy for retired investors to grasp and feel comfortable with. The multiple asset classes reduce the risk of loss due to poor performance in any given segment of the financial markets, while providing the opportunity to profit in additional areas that may be overlooked. Examples of some of these asset classes would include mid-sized global companies, global bonds, and real estate.

The bottom line is to ask your financial professional how you are diversified and how many asset classes you own. If your investments are all in Canadian stocks and you hold three balanced funds that all invest in Canadian stocks, you may consider diversifying to minimize the risk of concentration in one area.

Another question to ask is whether your investments are rebalanced on an ongoing basis to manage risk and, if so, how they are rebalanced. Ask for an example. You should receive comfort in the knowledge that your money is being rebalanced to take advantage of opportunities and to prevent over- or under-weighting in specific asset classes, which could lead to undesirable volatility or fluctuations of your money or risk. This may answer your question about how you are diversified.

Every generation laughs at the old fashions, but religiously follows the new.
Henry David Thoreau

Nothing can bring you peace but yourself.
Ralph Waldo Emerson

Mistake 6

NO SYSTEM FOR REBALANCING YOUR PORTFOLIO ON A REGULAR BASIS

Rebalancing Tires and Money

In Canada, we all know the importance of maintaining our vehicles for winter. Having come from Winnipeg, I have the habit of putting on the snow tires, bringing out the storm windows, and preparing for the cold weather. Living on Vancouver Island changes the need for snow tires, but we still need to regularly rotate our tires for maintenance and efficiency. How about your portfolio? How is it rebalanced?

Avoid the pitfalls faced by investors–market volatility, currency risks, rising interest rates, and missed opportunities. Rebalancing on a regular basis can help you stay on track and on the road when things get rough. There are six ways to establish a rebalancing program with your finances. These types of rebalancing can help preserve your capital. The types of rebalancing, or what I refer to as elements of diversification, are:

1. Periodic (monthly, quarterly, or annual) adjustment of your portfolio mix.

2. Threshold, as in percentage-based, such as 5% to 8% off target.

3. Range-based, which adjusts your investments back to certain limits rather than a fixed asset allocation.

4. Volatility-based, which takes into account the expected range of ups and downs due to markets and types of holdings (high- or low-risk).

5. Active, which is determined based on markets and results.

6. Dynamic, which may use a combination of the different types of rebalancing strategies in a systematic way to achieve capital preservation.

Most pension plans in Canada utilize rebalancing strategies to preserve the capital for retirees and maintain payouts based on market conditions. Rebalancing your money can keep you safely on the road to financial success.

Happiness does not depend on outward things, but on the way we see them.
Leo Tolstoy

The art of living lies less in eliminating our troubles than in growing with them.
Bernard M. Baruch

Mistake 7
NOT MANAGING RISK

How to Utilize Diversification to Manage Your Money

There are more investment management programs available
for Canadians today than ever before. There are now several
different opportunities for investors to diversify their portfolios
through managed programs, which used to be designed only for
the wealthy investor in North America. Larry Herscu wrote a
book entitled *The Canadian Guide to Managed Accounts* (WRAP
Publications, January, 2004), which gives Canadians true insight
into some of the leading-edge diversification programs available
to investors.

Understanding the benefits of these programs comes down to a few
simple tenets. First, if you realize that almost 90% of your return
comes from diversification of your assets–for example, by asset
class, geography, market capitalization, and investment style–then
portfolio-managed programs may be for you. Second, rebalancing
or adjusting your portfolio to market conditions to minimize risk
and maximize returns in the best possible way takes a team of expert
managers. The rebalancing is what most investors are missing. Third,
teams of professionals and pension style managers–who manage
millions for pension plans and private institutions–can be accessed
today. They can manage your money in the same manner that successful pension plans are managed. Finally, you get three sets of eyes
looking over your portfolio–the investment manager(s), the portfolio
rebalancing and review team, and your advisor–all working to make
sure you have ongoing, appropriate diversification. And with several
portfolio options from which to choose in Canada, managed programs are helping more and more Canadians invest in programs that
are tailored for them. Find out or ask about managed programs.

Remember to read and review the simplified prospectus and appropriate merits, and disclaimers, of each program.

The shortest way to do many things is to do only one thing at a time.
Richard Cech

Imagination is more important than knowledge.
Albert Einstein

Mistake 8
THE WRONG TIME HORIZON

Average life expectancy increased from 47 years in 1900 to almost 78 in 2004. Do not underestimate how long you might be around. The tables show that it could be longer rather than shorter, so consider investing your funds accordingly. Have you ever had the thought or concern, "Do I have enough money to last?"

When people get concerned about preserving money, having enough of it, and wanting to keep it close to the vest, what types of investments do they often make? Usually lower-yielding investments. Instead of looking at other investment options including annuities, income funds, or mid- to long-term GICs, they keep their investment capital in a short-term, cashable GIC, or even worse, a low- or no-interest bank account.

If you can earn higher returns on a longer-term GIC, why would you buy the short-term GIC? My response is that with the short-term GIC the return is good for six months, after which you have the option of reinvesting your money in another GIC or any other investment vehicle you choose. Although the return might be lower, these shorter-term investments facilitate the need for liquidity better than the long-term GIC.

On the other hand, longer-term fixed-income securities typically provide for a higher income, which can be helpful in meeting current needs. For these reasons, it is very important to consider, before you put your plan in place, the trade-off between your living needs and your potential need for liquidity.

Everyone's goals are different. As people age and get older, they might think that they should invest for a shorter and shorter time horizon because they are getting older. In some cases, this can be a big mistake. In a lot of cases, I advise that investments should outlast one's life expectancy.

Ultimately, either you are going to out-live your money or your money is going to out-live you. Assuming you have the financial ability to make this choice, I should think you would rather have your money out-live you.

Statistics suggest that a person who reaches the age of 73 will live another 14 years on average. Assuming that life expectancies stay the same or increase and your life expectancy follows that of the average person, your portfolio at age 73 might need to keep working for an average of 14 years. Therefore, if you want your money to last as long as you do, wouldn't it make sense to consider investment strategies to help you meet your living needs for another 14 years instead of 6 months or 12 months?

Fortify yourself with contentment, for this is an impregnable fortress.
Epictetus

Happiness depends more on the inward disposition of mind than on outward circumstances.
Benjamin Franklin

Mistake 9
LETTING EMOTIONS DRIVE YOUR INVESTMENT DECISIONS

Testing Your Emotions

It is a well known fact that 80% of professional money managers under-perform their relevant indexes. Even worse, a large percentage of investors lose money even when investing in mutual funds that out-perform their relevant indexes. Between 1980 and 1992 the most successful fund in the United States compounded annually at more than 25%, yet most investors lost money. How is this possible? The average investor held the fund for seven months. Being raised in Manitoba, a prairie province, I know that you cannot plant seeds in August and expect a wonderful crop in September. It takes patience and time. Yet with so much instant information available to us everyday, we evaluate our returns on a daily and weekly basis. Can you imagine if you did this with your home? Imagine coming home from a hard day's work and turning on the TV or computer and evaluating the price of your home. Sounds crazy doesn't it? Yet so many investors do this on a daily basis. One would think that access to more information should make one a better investor, right?

Successful investors will agree that these erratic emotions and acions are rooted in the psychological forces that seem to under-lie most of the poor results. Warren Buffett, known as one of the world's greatest investors, once said, "To invest successfully over a lifetime does not require a stratospheric IQ, unusual business insight, or inside information. What is needed is a sound intellectual framework for decisions and the ability to keep emotions from corroding that framework." Mr. Buffett is absolutely right. The fact is, we all want instant gratification; and investing is no different. We want returns without risk or time. We don't want volatility yet we want consistency. We don't want to do exactly the wrong thing at exactly the right time. So the next time you read your statement, or watch the financial news, ask yourself what you are really trying to accomplish here. What is your expected annual return averaged over a five-year period (not annually or, worse, weekly or daily)?

Have faith in businesses, not the stock market. If I were to ask you about how your investments are performing, could you tell me? Does it give you comfort or concern? Does thinking about it bother you? Clearly, you are not in control of the stock markets. Take control of your emotions and your plan today. Plan for less risk or volatility, if you are concerned. One of Warren Buffet's mentors was a successful investor and writer, Benjamin Graham.

The Short Story of Benjamin Graham

Known as one of the greatest investment advisors of all time, Ben Graham wrote the timeless and classic money management book *The Intelligent Investor* (Harper Business Essentials). As we head into summer holidays, I can't help but re-read this book of wisdom. Originally published in 1949, *The Intelligent Investor* provides emotional strategies and analytical insight that are essential to financial success. Every successful money manager on the planet uses this book as a true reference and follows the principles it contains.

Born in 1894, Graham is known as the father of value investing. Despite the dramatic stock market crash and 70% losses of 1929 through 1932, Graham survived and found the true spirit of value investing. Some of the core principles Graham developed were:

Invest for profits. An investor would not normally buy a business that did not, on proper research, appear to have a reasonable expectation of producing good profits over time. Share investors should take the same approach and buy, as Graham says, "...not on optimism, but on arithmetic."

The future value of every investment is a function of its present price. The higher the price you pay, the lower your return will be.

No matter how cautious, the one risk you cannot eliminate is being wrong. Minimize your risk by what Graham called your margin of safety. For Benjamin Graham, the benchmark for calculating the margin of safety was the interest rate payable for prime quality bonds.

Become an investor, not a speculator. The difference is that an investor is one who invests in an operation which, through thorough analysis, promises safety of one's principal and a return. Operations not meeting these requirements are speculative. The secret to success, he said, is inside you. By developing your discipline, you can ignore other people and the media and govern your own financial success. In the end, how your investments behave is much less important than how you behave.

You're happiest while you're making the greatest contribution.
Robert F. Kennedy

There is more to life than increasing its speed.
Mahatma Ghandi

Mistake 10
NOT DOING WHAT THE RICH DO

Today's wealthy investors are usually very involved in their financial matters. There is a tremendous amount of information available today on wealth management. Russ Alan Prince recently published *Wealth Management* (Wealth Management Press 2003) and defines it as "delivering a full range of investment and advanced planning services and products to affluent people." Prince describes advanced planning for the wealthy in four areas including "Wealth Enhancement, Wealth Transfer, Asset Protection, and Charitable Giving."

Wealth enhancement deals with taxation. What the rich do well is learn the strategies to minimize tax, such as use of dividend and capital gains income, systematic withdrawal programs, asset swaps, trusts, tax shelters, and advanced strategies to defer taxation.

Wealth transfer is more than just writing out a will. Joint meetings with your advisor and lawyer accomplish more in less time. It is a team approach the rich strive for. Using planning strategies such as life insurance beneficiary designations, life insurance and annuity contracts, spousal trusts, and segregated funds can help accomplish wealth transfer and peace of mind.

Asset protection is defined as protecting your capital and knowing safe strategies for minimizing risk of loss. These losses can include market fluctuations as well as protection from creditors, ex-spouses, or family members. The strategies can be directly related to the risk of a challenge from another party or a function of recognizing risk tolerance and appropriately matching your investments and portfolio asset allocation.

Charitable giving can be more than just giving money. Several successful people in this great community donate their time and efforts to giving back. From a monetary point, the rich clearly want to give something back, sometimes with or without fanfare or prestige. Did you know that you can easily set up your own individual or family foundation? Strategies for charitable giving can include foundations, charitable tax planning, and charitable trusts. The rich do more planning with their teams. They are like Lieutenant Columbo asking, "...just one more question."

Can you imagine that some companies have only four to six investment models? Attempting to use a conservative/balanced/moderate-growth/aggressive platform is the same as saying that every consumer fits neatly into one of only five models. I believe that's silly.

That's why you should consider goals-based retirement planning. Each goal has a specific investment mix, so you may have several different portfolio needs–all with specific risk tolerances. For example, say Fred and Wilma from Parksville are retired and want money for large trips or cruises. They also need money available for the executor of their estate, and they want to put away some money for their grandchildren. The rest is to use for income in their retirement. Some of their money is in nonregistered investments outside RRSPs and some money is in RRSPs.

They have four or five specific goals. All of these categories have specific investment risks and time horizons. To put them all in one big investment model just doesn't cut it. Yet, many companies do it that way. Why?

Managed asset programs usually offer more than sixty investment portfolios, each featuring a very specific, highly detailed asset allocation model for specific needs and goals. But which portfolios are right for you? Each goal is customized to your unique needs.

For Fred and Wilma, let's say the investment portfolio for the grandchildren is higher risk and has a 15-year time frame because of the age of the grandkids. Then they can build the investment for the specific goal, different from their own retirement income objectives, which may have some short-term needs and longer-term targets depending on their ages. There is no guarantee that a specific portfolio will meet that objective but having one portfolio for multiple objectives definitely brings more worry than goals-based retirement planning, which is to build a few specific portfolios for each goal or need. Consider asking your investment professional to develop goals-based retirement planning for your specific needs.

Action may not always bring happiness, but there is no happiness without action.
Benjamin Disraeli

Great effort from great motives is the best definition of a happy life.
William Ellery Channing

Mistake 11
GENERATING A LOW YIELD WHEN YOU NEED MORE INCOME

Increasing Your Average Yield

Given the situation in the world today, fixed-term products are enjoying resurgence in popularity as more and more people look for ways to diversify portfolios with reliable, income-producing investments. For those who want higher rates without risk or loss of principal, there are options that offer attractive returns. One simple method of guaranteeing the return of your principal, while providing the opportunity to participate in the market, blends the safety of a GIC with the growth advantages of a mutual fund.

Begin by purchasing a monthly or annual interest GIC. Return of principal is guaranteed at maturity as long as deposit insurance rules are observed. Deposit the interest into the mutual fund of your choice to achieve the advantage of dollar cost averaging during the term of the GIC. First, project the amount you'd need to invest in a compounding GIC in order to get your principal back at maturity. Second, invest the difference in a mutual fund. At the end of the term, you have return of principal plus an income component made up of the mutual fund of your choice. For example: suppose you had $50,000 to invest for 5 years at 5%. You don't want to risk the $50,000 but feel the market has potential for growth. You purchase a GIC in the amount of $39,176.31, which grows to $50,000 in five years. The remaining $10,823.69 is invested in a mutual fund. If the mutual fund averages 10% per annum over five years, you will have a total of $67,431.66, and the average annual yield on the total investment would be 6.164%. In times of uncertainty, your best bet is to create a plan that fits your particular needs and stick with it.

Guaranteeing an Increase in Your Income

For the retiree who wants it all—no risk, high income, and low taxes—an insured annuity appeals to thousands.

Most people have never heard of this investment option, yet thousands of Canadians set up insured annuities each year for a guaranteed retirement plan.

An insured annuity will provide you with a guaranteed income and preserve the capital for your heirs. The insured annuity is made up of two components, a prescribed annuity and a life insurance policy. The prescribed annuity provides a guaranteed source of income for each year of retirement, with the income made up of a combination of a return of capital investment and interest earned on that investment. Only the interest component of the annual annuity income is taxable. Since this is a prescribed annuity, the taxable amount is averaged over the life of the annuity. Both of these factors help to maximize after-tax return. The insurance provides tax-free funds to heirs on your death, replacing the capital used to fund retirement.

Insured annuities will appeal to those who are about age 60 or more, who have nonregistered capital to invest, who prefer high, long-term guaranteed rates of return, who have assets in GICs, and who are insurable (healthy).

If you are looking for a part of your retirement capital and estate to be guaranteed, take a closer look at insured annuities.

Happiness is where we find it, but rarely where we seek it.
J. Petit Senn

Happiness depends upon ourselves.
Aristotle

Mistake 12
NOT MANAGING YOUR RETIREMENT NEST EGG LIKE A PENSION PLAN

Can Anyone–Even You–Buy a Pension Plan?

Buying a pension plan sounds like a great plan for your retirement, but what does a pension plan do with your money? How do they invest it? What will you get when you retire?

Without going into a long article on how pension plans work, the one thing people are after is retirement income for that fateful day when they can say goodbye to work and hello to retirement, as long as they have enough income.

But what if you're already retired? How can you invest and generate income like a pension plan? The word "pension" is defined in the dictionary as an allowance, annuity, or benefit. So how can you benefit? Here are a few ideas.

First, a pension plan invests money like a balanced mutual fund. Roughly half is invested into stocks and the other half into fixed-income investments such as bonds, mortgages, etc. If you want to invest like a pension plan, find a consistent conservative balanced fund and you instantly have an investment similar to a pension plan. Second, if you're already retired, invest into a balanced fund and take out income on a regular basis. Some balanced funds are called "growth and income" and some are called "income." They are designed like pension plans; in fact, some of the managers are pension plan managers as well. They understand pension plans, so they manage the fund like a pension plan. A third way to benefit is to invest into an annuity. An annuity gives you monthly income for life. There are also ways to set up annuities so there is money or income for your spouse and estate. To ease your retirement planning worries, consider the merits of buying your own pension plan.

Look Beyond Mutual Funds

One day Ed from Qualicum dropped by to ask about wrap accounts.

"Grant," he said in a loud voice, "what's all this noise about wealth management and these programs? It seems to be the hot topic in investing today. Is it?"

"Well Ed, knowing that you're from Alberta originally, people such as yourself don't usually go around saying they're wealthy, but some have been able to accumulate savings of more than $500,000 in their working years and want to invest their hard-earned money in a manner that is in alignment with their goals."

Ed fired back saying, "Do you mean to tell me that if I have a bunch of money, investment companies will treat me differently?"

My reply was that pooled funds, also known as managed accounts or wrap accounts, differ from traditional mutual funds.

"How so?" he asked.

"First of all, pooled funds have higher minimums; so the larger investors can customize their accounts to their specific investment goals, risk tolerances, and time horizons. These funds include daily portfolio monitoring and rebalancing, strategic tax planning, and the flexibility to offset capital gains and losses. An individual mutual fund is not as complex."

Ed leaned forward and asked the key question, "Why isn't everyone doing this?

My reply was simple. "They are doing it, Ed. Most companies in Canada have programs, several programs in fact; and minimums can be as low as $25,000 or as high as more than $1 million. In the United States over $400 billion is invested this way. Most mutual fund companies today have a wide array of offerings, including pooled funds. Heck, Ed, you may be able to switch some of your existing funds into a customized program without any switching cost, but doing so may trigger income tax."

Ed now understands pooled funds versus mutual funds. This is a great way to build a pension plan in retirement. It is called a multi-manager approach.

Ask your financial professional if this is the way for you to go. Think differently in retirement.

Opportunity is missed by most people because it is dressed in overalls and looks like work.
Thomas Edison

Go confidently in the direction of your dreams. Live the life you've imagined.
Henry David Thoreau

Mistake 13

NOT UNDERSTANDING THE MOST POWERFUL INVESTMENT EVER

Once in a while I have the opportunity to teach finance in a school setting. I talk about four things one can do with one's money–spend, save, invest, and donate.

Spending and saving do not need much explanation, but I do explain that investing and saving are two very different principles. Saving has a short-term cycle, while investing holds the value and grows or maintains and generates income.

Finally we come to donate. It's the one thing some of the wealthiest people on the planet have done and are doing. It's the one thing written about in various ancient cultures and still promoted today. It's the one thing that brings money to anyone who does it, yet at the same time most people fear doing it. Donating does not have to be in cash money. Look at all of the wonderful volunteers in the community and around the world donating their time. After all, time is money. This is one of the greatest money-making secrets in history: Give money or time away. That's right. Give it away. Give it to people who help you, inspire you, heal you, or move you. Give without expecting it to be returned; it will come back to you multiplied from some source.

In 1924 John D. Rockefeller wrote to his son and explained his practice of giving away money. He wrote, "...in the beginning of getting money, away back in my childhood, I began giving it away, and continued increasing the gifts as the income increased..." He gave away more money as he received more income. He gave away $550 million dollars in his lifetime. We see it every day in our community, businesses giving to worthy causes. But what I'm talking about here is individual giving. I'm talking about you giving money so you will receive more money. Give something from your heart. Don't be stingy.

Come from abundance, not scarcity. Give without expecting return. As you do, you will see your own prosperity grow.

Who is your beneficiary on your RRSPs or RRIFs? Did you know you can designate more than one person and you can include a charity? For income tax purposes, a charitable donation made under a will is deemed to have been made immediately before death. Accordingly, the donation can qualify for the charitable donation tax credit in the year of death. Furthermore, to the extent it is not claimed in the year of death, the charitable credit can be carried back and claimed in the preceding year.

Until recently, where an individual designated a charity as a beneficiary under a RRSP or RRIF, the gift did not qualify for the charitable tax credit. The credit upon death was available only with respect to donations that were stipulated in the will–and direct designations under RRSPs and RRIFs did not meet this requirement.

Fortunately, the Government has changed the rules, and the tax credit is now available for gifts to charities that are made by way of a direct designation under a RRSP or RRIF. As a result, the credit in these circumstances will be available in the year of death or in the preceding year, as described above. These changes apply to deaths occurring after 1998.

The amount of the donation for these purposes will generally be the fair market value, determined by the time of death, of the gift from the RRSP or RRIF. The gift must actually be made to the charity within 36 months of the death, although the CRA has the discretion to extend this period. Note that a similar new rule will allow the charitable tax credit when a charity is designated as a direct beneficiary under a life insurance policy.

If you are looking for ways to plan your estate, leave the nontaxable assets to the family and the taxable assets, such as RRSPs and RRIFs, to a charity. This may maximize your estate; however, professional advice should always be considered when planning your estate.

Important note, please read: Any charitable donation should be discussed with your legal and tax representatives, as part of your overall financial and estate plan, before you make any decision, since they will have up to date information as tax and legal rules change. Professional advice should always be sought before making any financial or charitable decision.

Persistence is to the character of man as carbon is to steel.
Napoleon Hill

Try not to do too many things at once. Know what you want, the number one thing today and tomorrow. Persevere and get it done.
George Allen

Mistake 14
NOT USING THE SERVICES OF A DEPOSIT BROKER

What is a Deposit Broker?

Deposit brokers are independent retailers of financial products and services specializing in "guaranteed" investment products such as GICs, term deposits, and Canada Savings Bonds. They work diligently to provide you with the best independent advice on information affecting your deposit product needs. Deposit brokers maintain daily information on current interest rates, help you achieve the best possible return on your deposit investment, and work on your behalf to find the best investment available from all financial institutions including trust companies, banks, insurance and fund companies. And best of all, there is no fee for this service!

How do I Know My Deposit is Safe?

Recently, I have been asked a lot of questions about the safety of investments. Deposit insurance is available for qualifying deposits. Banks, trust companies, and mortgage and loan companies must be members of the Canadian Deposit Insurance Corporation (CDIC) or Credit Union Deposit Insurance Corporation (CUDIC). Deposits are insured up to $100,000 with banks and trust companies and unlimited with BC credit unions. Check your provincial guide for credit union deposit insurance. Life and health insurance companies can be members of the Canadian Life and Health Insurance Compensation Corporation (CompCorp, now called Assuris), which also insures deposits. Published listings of these member institutions may change from time to time due to corporate name changes, buyouts, or amalgamations.

There are limits to insurance protection, and not all deposits are insured. Certain terms and conditions may apply. For example, the maximum deposit term covered by CDIC is five years; there is no such limitation under CompCorp (Assuris). For detailed information on deposit insurance coverage, contact your financial institution.

What Type of Financial Products are Available Through a Deposit Broker?

Most deposit brokers are full-service investment advisors offering a complete range of financial products and services including: term deposits, guaranteed investment certificates, short-term deposits, cashable certificates, RRSPs, RRIFs, LIFs, annuities, mutual funds, and life insurance. You can get the best rates and widest selection of investment options at no cost to you by using the services of a deposit broker. Deposit brokers, unlike most investment advisors, have access to large-volume deposit product selections. Financial institutions use the deposit brokerage channel to offer these deals which can then be offered to investors efficiently and at top returns, completely free of fees or commission. A deposit broker receives compensation directly from the financial institution. To find out more, contact your financial advisor.

To find out how you can invest safely and with additional financial institutions, you can contact each institution and find someone to help you, or you can call a deposit broker, who deals with most banks, trust companies, and insurance companies. Contact the Registered Deposit Brokers Association <www.rdba.ca> for more information.

Why Can Deposit Brokers Offer Higher Rates Than Other Financial Institutions or Advisors?

Deposit brokers receive daily information on current interest rates and current product availability from financial institutions all across the country. The demand, volume, and availability of product vary daily and by institution, creating opportunities for better rates. These can be best accessed by a deposit broker working to understand investor needs and the best possible product solutions. Retirees on Vancouver Island like deposit brokers because of convenience and consolidation of investments on one statement (while diversifying through different institutions). In addition they find great rates on their deposits and, most importantly, keep their money safe.

Good News for GIC Investors

Canadians have an increased level of deposit insurance thanks to the 2005 Federal budget. The amount of deposit insurance coverage in CDIC member institutions has risen to $100,000. "We are very pleased that this increased level of deposit insurance protection is now available to Canadian consumers," said Guy Saint-Pierre, President and CEO of CDIC. CDIC, a Crown corporation, provides insurance to depositors against the loss, in whole or in part, of deposits made at member institutions in the event of their failure. The maximum basic coverage that is available for all eligible deposits that are held in the name of a depositor at a single member institution is $100,000 (principal and interest combined). CDIC provides separate coverage (up to a maximum of $100,000, including principal and interest) for each of the following types of eligible deposits:

-Those held jointly, in the name of two or more persons.

-Those held in trust.

-Those held in RRSPs or RRIFs.

This means that if you have a joint account, a RRSP account, and a RRIF account with one financial institution, you could have up to $300,000 insured through that single institution.

To be eligible for CDIC deposit insurance protection, deposits must be in Canadian currency, payable in Canada; repayable no later than five years from the date of deposit; and placed at a financial institution that is a CDIC member.

Some types of deposits and investments offered by member institutions are NOT insurable by CDIC. Among the most common types are:

-Foreign currency deposits (for example, accounts in US dollars).

-Term deposits that mature more than five years after the date of deposit.

-Debentures issued by banks.

-Treasury bills.

-Mutual funds.

-Stocks.

-Investments in mortgages.

For more information, contact your financial institution or visit <www.cdic.ca>.

What this power is I cannot say; all I know is that it exists and it becomes available only when a man is in that state of mind in which he knows exactly what he wants and is fully determined not to quit until he finds it.
Alexander Graham Bell

There is no chance, no destiny, no fate, that can hinder or control the firm resolve
of a determined soul.
Ella Wheeler Wilcox

Mistake 15
INVESTING IN DIVIDEND GROWTH INSTEAD OF DIVIDEND INCOME

Dividend Income or Growth?

A long time ago I was introduced to an investment strategy that
has stood the test of time in Canada. It is investing for income, in
particular dividend income. If the dividend increases over time then
so will the income. So often investors find themselves chasing growth
funds when they really want consistency and stability and sometimes
regular income. This is the case with dividend funds.

A dividend fund is a portfolio of companies or securities that pay
dividends, or profits from companies, to shareholders like you and
me. You see, most dividend funds are more or less stock funds that
are not designed for retirement income. Some dividend funds have
marginal dividend payouts but boast big returns.

Do you want growth or income? Do you want high returns or a
steady stream of cash flow and stability?

Planning your retirement income can be confusing when you are
reviewing your options. Dividend funds can hold a combination of
stocks, bonds, preferred shares, income trusts, and income-related
securities. Even the names can be confusing. Some are dividend
income funds, yet the income is marginal.

Finding the top-performing dividend fund does not mean you
are going to receive monthly income either. If your goal is to
look for tax-efficient dividend income, carefully sort through the
category of dividend funds and look at the types of holdings, not
the past performance. You will always find a dividend growth fund
performing better than a dividend income fund. But if stability of
your money and cash flow are important to your retirement income

plan, ignore the high-returning growth funds and look to consistent dividend, income-performing, funds or portfolios.

It is always safer to know what you own than to rely on the fund manager. He or she will never sit down with you to find out your goals, and to see if you need income or growth. A recent survey shows there are more than 160 different dividend funds. When it comes to dividend funds, check the prospectus and annual report or ask your financial professional the details of income or growth.

Don't let go of your dreams. If you have determination and belief in your dreams, you will succeed in spite of your desire to let go.
Catherine Pulsifer

Most of the important things in the world have been accomplished by people who have kept on trying when there seemed to be no help at all.
Dale Carnegie

Mistake 16
NOT AVOIDING HIGH-INCOME RISKS

Some retirees are not aware of all of their opportunities for a regular fixed income, or they misunderstand the income investments they already own. For example, many have purchased income mutual funds but these can lack two features that many retirees seek–a fixed regular income and return of principal at maturity.

Since income mutual funds may change their dividend payments at any time, the payments are often not fixed. Also, since mutual funds have no maturity date, the return of principal is not assured. Finding out how some income funds or portfolios calculate the monthly payout can be confusing. Some pay out a return of capital while others pay out mostly interest income. Some pay out dividend income and others pay out capital gains. Some may claim they are tax-efficient, but at what risk to your capital?

Examine the fund's record over the past five years. Is it consistent year after year, or does it all depend on the manager's discretion and performance? This will help separate the riskier income investments from those that are more conservative and consistent. If they have a solid component of interest income, they are likely to be holding bonds that have monthly or quarterly interest payments. These payments will be more predictable and less volatile, and they will provide comfort in the knowledge that they have a more regular income pattern.

Whether you are investing in stocks, bonds, or mutual funds, always make sure to do your homework first. If you are considering an investment in any type of mutual fund, carefully consider investment objectives, risks, charges, and expenses before investing. For this and other information about any mutual fund investment, always obtain a prospectus and read it carefully before you invest. Find out how the income payout is calculated so you understand what to expect, or ask your financial advisor.

Do or do not. There is no try.
Yoda

As I grow older, I pay less attention to what men say. I just watch what they do.
Andrew Carnegie

Mistake 17
NOT DIVERSIFYING INVESTMENTS

Joe Millionaire's Retirement Income Plan

Joe from Nanoose Bay dropped by to update me on his retirement income plan and to let me know he's on track. He has a retirement income plan that is suitable for a 65-year-old senior with a conservative investment focus.

Joe splits his investments up five ways. First, 20% is invested into one- and five-year GICs. Called a "barbell" approach, this invests half into short-term investments and half into long-term investments, taking advantage of averaging interest rates. The next 40% is invested into fixed income. This consists of a portfolio of bonds and bond funds including Government bonds, real-return bonds, high-yield bonds, and preferred shares. Joe likes the consistency of his fixed income portfolio and safety of GICs, since he had about 60% overall invested into conservative and less choppy (volatile) investments. The next 20% is in income trust funds, which invest into income-generating investments to give a monthly income. These consist of oil and gas, resource trusts, real estate, and business trusts. Joe likes the fact that the income is less taxing than interest income and that the strong oil and gas price and rise in real estate helps offset inflation. The final 20% produces income by being invested into dividend income pooled funds, stock funds that invest in companies that pay strong dividends. The dividend payout also gives Joe additional monthly income. Each section of his portfolio is designed to pay out income on a monthly or quarterly basis.

Joe wants to retain most of his capital and occasionally dips into principal to go on his expensive holidays. In five years, Joe wants to decrease the 40% equity to 20% and hopefully spend more on his travels. He is comfortable with the diversification into five asset areas. That way he can see from where his income will be generated, the specific dollar amounts of cash flow coming in, and what he can typically expect from each asset class. Now Joe can spend more time planning his next big trip accordingly.

Building an Income Portfolio

"How can you generate sufficient income to match my income needs and risk tolerance?"

This question was asked by Bob from Nanoose Bay. His situation is similar to that of many retirees faced with income needs at a time when stock markets remain uncertain and interest rates are low. Bob needs about $550 per month or 6.6% to supplement his income. He has $100,000 to invest. Unfortunately, we can't get him 6.6% in a term deposit. So we discussed looking for the highest-yielding term deposits, which are around 4.7% (rates subject to change)–well short of his required 6.6%.

Then we discussed other options such as corporate bonds, Government bonds, income trusts, dividend funds, and balanced funds. While he wants the income, Bob really wants an income portfolio. Based on his conservative risk tolerance he doesn't mind taking some risk. We then looked at some model income portfolios and their risks and came up with some possible portfolio options. Each portfolio is structured differently in the amount of risk and in the amount of tax he will pay (interest, dividend income, or capital gains income).

Here are some examples of simple mutual fund structures he can develop for his income portfolio:

-50% Federal and Provincial bonds and 50% corporate bonds.

-50% term deposits and 50% corporate bonds.

-33% preferred equities, 33% income trusts, and 33% dividend-paying common equities.

-25% corporate bonds, 25% preferred equities, 25% income trusts, and 25% dividend paying common equities.

The income trusts used in these examples consist of a fund that invests in 25% business trusts, 25% real estate investment trusts, 25% resource trusts, and 25% utility trusts.

Now Bob understands that, by combining lower-risk income options with potentially higher-return income options, he can generate income for his retirement that can match his risk tolerance and monthly cash flow. He can also look at existing portfolios that are designed to generate income and preserve capital for investors and see that over his time horizon, he can achieve his financial goals.

Get excited and enthusiastic about your own dream. This excitement is like a forest fire—you can smell it, taste it, and see it from a mile away.
Denis Waitley

You can do anything if you have enthusiasm. Enthusiasm is the yeast that makes your hopes rise to the stars. With it, there is accomplishment. Without it there are only alibis.
Henry Ford

Mistake 18
HEEDING HYSTERIA IN THE HEADLINES

Throughout history, people associated with the stock market loved predicting doom and gloom. They still do. Disaster lurks around every corner and, most important, is easy to sell. Read a selection of predictions from the beginning of the printed word until today, and you'll be amazed that anyone is alive, much less prospering! Take a look at some of these actual forecasts, predictions, and headlines about the stock market from the past:

Don't fall for it when they tell you—buy now! Prices are going higher! Because prices are heading for one of the worst plunges you've ever seen. (1951, Dow Jones Industrial Average: 262)

Will this major shake-up in America's wealth wipe out your savings and cripple your future? (1954, Dow Jones Industrial Average: 330)

USSR launches Sputnik 1, US dominance in doubt, Dow off almost 10% in under a month. (1957, Dow Jones Industrial Average: 419)

Cuban missile crisis jams indexes sharply lower. (1962, Dow Jones Industrial Average: 590)

Increased Vietnam bombings and talk of high taxes rout markets. (1966, Dow Jones Industrial Average: 785)

Nixon resignation, runaway inflation, and the crisis of confidence in the economy forever change the market. (1974, Dow Jones Industrial Average: 616)

Joe Granville's "abandon all hope" message sparks a giant sell-off on record volume. (1981, Dow Jones Industrial Average: 875)

Is it 1929 all over again? Huge bear market feared. (1987, Dow Jones Industrial Average: 1,805)

Our expectation is that we are facing a long bear market, perhaps as long as five years, and that a great part of the advance of the past 15 years will be retraced in that time. (1990, Dow Jones Industrial Average: 2,670)

Is this the end? Three savvy pros look at the bear that's begun. (1994, Dow Jones Industrial Average: 3,762)

Professor's sophisticated computer model forecasts 40 % decline for equities. (1996, Dow Jones Industrial Average: 5,354)

If you're not prepared for the bear, you risk getting mauled. (1997, Dow Jones Industrial Average: 6,703)

Market forecast looks grim. (2003, Dow Jones Industrial average 8850)

I'll bet that, at the time they ran, these headlines and predictions had the desired effect and scared the bejesus out of people. The best way for you to short-circuit the panic you will inevitably feel over the course of your investment program is to focus on all the other panics and their aftermath. Remember that not even the great crash and depression of the 1930s would have destroyed a long-term investor who stuck with a superior investment strategy. (From *How to Retire Rich* by James O'Shaughnessy.)

The Day Warren Buffett Lost $342 Million

Hey, seen any positive headlines lately? It's human nature to feel nervous at times like these. You're not alone. The ONLY way to persevere through short-term volatility is to take the long-term view. I repeat, take the long-term view. Study and look at history. Look at five- and ten-year numbers; examine markets over longer periods; and remember, we've been through this before.

Think back to the crash of 1987. Warren Buffett, one of the richest men on the planet, owned a company called Berkshire Hathaway Inc. On Friday, October 16, 1987, his company was worth $3,890 per share. On the close of business on Monday, October 19, 1987, Berkshire was worth $3,180 per share. That day he lost $342 million worth of the value of his company, except that he really didn't lose it. How, you ask? Well, he never sold it. He waited patiently, and he more than recovered the loss. Today his company trades at more than $64,000 US dollars for one share (symbol BRK).

The lesson here is that the rich have been here before. If you want to find a recipe for success, Mr. Buffett is one of the best examples that you will find. I'm sure Mr. Buffett felt nervous and anxious back then; however, he was lucky. He didn't have the constant media, news, internet ticker, stock channel, etc., reminding him every second of the state of the markets. The media has us so wired into watching–weekly, daily, hourly–these flashing green and red arrows. To give them credit, it sells; and just like coffee we are so hooked on it that we feel we need our daily dose. Admit it, it's ridiculous.

So what are you going to do about it? I understand the nervousness and concern, that's human nature. The way to persevere through short-term volatility is to create a game plan. Imagine the Vancouver Canucks going into the playoffs without a game plan. Create one for your time horizon. If it is five years, then focus five years ahead, not day to day.

I share Mr. Buffett's philosophy because it is one of the best examples of a disciplined investment philosophy called value investing. Mr. Buffett is also well documented through books, publications, and daily media coverage. He is known as the sage of Omaha–a man who does not own a computer, who does not invest in any technology stocks, and who has built his entire fortune through the stock market. He is good friends with Bill Gates of Microsoft but has never invested in Microsoft because he says he doesn't understand it. His company, Berkshire Hathaway, has compounded more than 20% since starting in 1969.

A few of his investment comments or insights can be considered rules for the value investor. Some of my favorites are:

Never invest in a business you cannot understand.

Buy companies with strong histories of profitability and with a dominant business franchise.

Be fearful when others are greedy and be greedy when others are fearful.

Much success can be attributed to inactivity–most investors cannot resist the temptation to constantly buy and sell. Lethargy bordering on sloth should remain the cornerstone of an investment style.

An investor should act as though he had a lifetime decision card with just twenty punches on it.

"Turnarounds" seldom turn.

Do not take yearly results seriously; focus instead on four- or five-year averages.

Look for companies with high profit margins.

Growth and value investing are joined at the hip.

Buy a business; don't rent stocks.

Wide diversification is only required when investors do not understand what they are doing.

Focus on return on equity, not earnings per share.

The critical investment factor is determining the intrinsic value of a business and paying a fair or bargain price.

It is optimism that is the enemy of the rational buyer.

Invest for the long term.

If you wish to learn more about Warren Buffet's incredible track record and how he applies his philosophy, check out <www. berkshirehathaway.com> or visit your local bookstore or library for several books written about him that I'm sure you will enjoy. Mr. Buffett concocted a great recipe for investing success.

Nothing great was ever achieved without enthusiasm.
Emerson

Throw your heart over the fence and the rest will follow.
Norman Vin

Mistake 19
LESS DIVERSIFICATION AND MORE WORRY

In his new and revealing book *The Empowered Investor*, portfolio manager Keith Matthews, having spent twenty years in the investment industry, offers some very practical advice. Here are some of his investment principles:

1. Realize that no one has an investment crystal ball, including stock market strategists, economists, or financial advisory firms. Ignore predictions; they are one of your obstacles. Concentrate on executing and maintaining the winning strategies in your portfolio.

2. Behavioral finance has shown that an investor's emotions can have a negative impact on investment results. Often, hype found in the media, financial service literature, or even in social settings might entice investors to make investment decisions that they will later regret.

3. Asset-class investing is the most important step in taking control of your investments, and it has a bigger impact on your portfolio than market timing or stock picking.

4. Most investors and many advisors misunderstand the concept of diversification. They believe that because they own 15 stocks or 10 mutual funds, they are diversified. Too much overlap equals bad diversification. Improper diversification can be a recipe for disaster.

5. Discover and use the Fama/French 3-factor model when constructing and designing your portfolio: Stocks outperform bonds; value stocks outperform growth stocks; small-company stocks outperform large-company stocks.

6. Execute your asset allocation with asset-class index tools. All tools are not built the same. Build your portfolio and work

with an independent advisor who is free to recommend the best tools in the marketplace—tools that are transparent, precise, tax-efficient, and flexible.

7. Write an investment policy statement (IPS). An IPS will keep you within your specified risk parameters and greatly enhance your investment experience.

8. Recognize that costs matter. Taxes, management fees, trading costs, and investment advisory fees have an impact on your long-term investment results. Know your costs of investing.

9. Investments and life work together, and a well-considered plan is crucial to ensure that your dreams become a financial viability.

10. Get on with your life.

Putting Together a New Mutual Fund Portfolio

You're retired, now what? You have a retirement nest egg and off you go to your local financial advisor for some recommendations. You have some well-known or not-so-well-known mutual funds that seem to have done well lately. You want to add to the mix, so you pick a few more winners.

That is exactly what many investors do year after year. Based on last year's performance, investors buy the hot-sheet funds published in magazines, in newspapers, or on Web sites. The problem is that if they all did well together, they will most likely also fall together.

The goal is diversification and managing risk. You see, when investments are performing well, risk can be added to your portfolio, since the investments' losses can be magnified as markets rise. Your risk increases as markets increase. Turn the newspaper upside down and try to find investments that under-performed your winners in the good times. That is where you may find bargains and opportunities.

Your goal should be selecting funds that are complementary, so that your portfolio consistently performs well year after year, instead of like a roller coaster. It may sound funny, but many investors sell the under-performing funds at the very time they should be adding to them. Asset allocation and professionally managed investment programs can assist you. They take the emotion and decision-making out of your hands and put them into those of a team of experts aiming for a consistent return.

Talk to your financial professionals to be sure your investments are diversified and can weather the downturns when markets go south, as they do from time to time. They have software programs that can analyze your portfolio to see if it needs further diversification instead of just selling under-performers and buying top performers. After all, with a financial newspaper or Web site, anyone can do that; but that might not be the right thing to do next time you have money to invest.

All our dreams can come true—if we have the courage to pursue them.
Walt Disney

If opportunity doesn't knock, build a door.
Milton Berle

Mistake 20
NOT MAXIMIZING YOUR CPP BENEFITS

Consider ways to maximize your Canada Pension Plan. This could include early retirement, contributing past age 60, and splitting or assigning CPP benefits to a spouse.

First, you need to know how much you are entitled to receive (and your spouse if you are married) as well as your net income for all sources (and that of your spouse). Your entitlement can be determined by a call to the CPP office, toll-free, at 800-959-8281. Your net income can be found on your income tax return statement.

Early Retirement

You are entitled to receive CPP at the age of 60. If you have contributed the maximum over your working life, you are probably better off receiving CPP early.

Although you will receive a reduced amount, inflation at 3% will probably offset any gain in your contributions if you wait until the age of 65 to receive them.

Contributing past the age of 60 may be beneficial if you are short one or two years of maximum pensionable earnings. This will assure the maximum available to you at the age of 65; otherwise you may never receive the maximum allowable to you. If you have missed more than three years' maximum contributions, then you will not receive the maximum. Your normal CPP benefits are based on a complex formula involving your inflation-adjusted pensionable earnings.

Splitting CPP with Your Spouse

Upon retirement, couples may assign up to 50% of their benefits to their spouses provided they are both at the age of 60. Under the *Income Tax Act* the attribution rules of giving income to your spouse to avoid taxes does not apply for CPP. For example, if Bob from Qualicum Beach retires with the maximum available and his income is higher than his spouse, Mary, he can assign half of his CPP benefit each year to Mary and lower his net taxable income. This is an effective technique to split income and can be simply done by completing a form available from Canada Revenue Agency (CRA).

Call 800-O-CANADA for more information, or you can visit the following website: <www.servicecanada.gc.ca>

Life's a voyage that's homeward bound.
Herman Melville

Chapter 2

MANAGE

BUILDING A RETIREMENT
INCOME PLAN AND INVESTMENT
STRATEGY

GRANT HICKS

Knowledge of what is possible is the beginning of happiness.
George Santayana

Mistake 21
JUST BUYING A MUTUAL FUND WHEN YOU CAN GO CORPORATE CLASS

If you are investing your hard-earned after-tax money in a mutual fund, I have one question for you. Is the mutual fund or segregated fund taxable on an annual basis; and if so, do you know how much tax you might pay this year on it?

Until recently, mutual fund investors did not have a choice, they had to pay the tax. However, some investment companies now separate mutual fund investors as taxable and tax-class. Mutual fund companies know investors have different investment needs and therefore have created two types, one called "mutual fund trusts" and the second called "corporate-class" or "tax-class" investments. The corporate-class investors have the luxury of deferring taxes until they sell the fund or portfolio or start to take out income. They also have a huge advantage in that they can switch to another mutual fund in the same class without triggering any tax. For example, if I switch from US Equity Class fund to Canadian Dividend Class fund, there is no tax. I am not stuck on switching my investments and diversifying because of tax.

Investors in regular mutual funds are always concerned about their after-tax annual returns, since some or all of the income generated may be taxable in the year received. Even worse, some investors purchase a mutual fund in November and receive taxable distributions from the fund in December as if they held it for a full year, potentially adding a lot of tax, yikes!

The other problem that can arise is if the fund manager has to decide on keeping or selling a security that has a large capital gain or one that has no capital gain. That is the same for the investor as the switching problem. If you go from an equity fund to a money market fund there may be a taxable capital gain; but if you go from equity- to short-term class, there is no tax. This investment structure offers investors more flexibility for their nonregistered money. The next time you talk to your advisor, ask whether your nonregistered investment can be separated between mutual funds and tax-class funds.

Defer Tax, Save Money Every Year

If you could invest outside of a RRSP and defer taxes, would you? If you could defer taxation on your investments until you decide to trigger the tax, would you? If you could turn interest income into capital gains income and keep the investment into bonds, would you?

If you answered yes to any of those questions, you need to learn about corporate-class mutual fund plans, which offer the ability to invest in a variety of mutual funds and defer taxation until the investor decides to withdraw the money. There are two tax structures under which mutual funds are set up. Most are established as mutual fund trusts; the others as mutual fund corporations.

Investing in mutual fund corporations provides several benefits, usually without additional cost. These benefits include tax deferral, tax-free switching, capital gains taxes on income, and options for diversification.

I had a friend that wanted to switch out of a fund that she held for more than ten years. The management of the fund changed, and she wasn't comfortable with the new direction. Her options were to pay the capital gain of more than $30,000 and switch to a new investment or leave it as is because she had such a large tax bill. It became a tax decision more than an investment decision.

By establishing funds inside a corporate share structure, you are eliminating this problem down the road, and you can make sound financial decisions regardless of the tax.

A second example is a market downturn. If an investor wants to switch to cash or to a short-term fund because of volatility, he or she can switch without any tax consequences.

A financial planning tip: I strongly recommend you examine the funds you own, figure out the capital gains and losses on switching these funds around today, then imagine if they were all in corporate share structures, which would eliminate the taxes upon switching. Several companies now offer corporate structures and most financial professionals usually only recommend corporate share funds for clients. As one investor put it to me, why would you not have all of your investments in corporate-class?

A Different Kind of Mutual Fund

One of the last things we need these days is another mutual fund. When I started in the financial business some sixteen years ago, there were approximately 400 different mutual funds. Now there are more than 5,000 in Canada alone.

There is another type that is not exactly a mutual fund. Let me explain. There are two tax structures under which mutual funds are set up. Most are mutual fund trusts. The second and newest type of structure is a mutual fund corporation. A fund company issues several classes of shares and calls them "funds," with each class of shares representing a different mutual fund. As an investor, you are permitted to switch among the share classes without triggering capital gains on those you previously owned. As long as your investment remains within the corporate share structure, capital gains earned on a specific class of share are deferred. In layman's terms, if you buy an equity fund under a corporate structure and switch it for another equity or short-term fund under the corporate structure, there is no tax or capital gain triggered, unlike a typical mutual fund.

If you don't own corporate funds outside your RRSP, now would be a good time to switch into them—examine the tax consequences first.

How Mr. Jones Kept Up with the Neighbors

Mr. Jones dropped by to discuss how he could protect his income from the market and Revenue Canada (now CRA).

Last year, Mr. Jones was uncomfortable holding stocks and mutual funds and decided to sell at a loss, triggering a capital loss. His argument to me was that at age 70 he might never be able to use up his capital losses because he could not see himself investing in the stock market for quite awhile.

"It's fine for my neighbors since they're in their fifties and have a long time to recover from market drops, so they will eventually reap the rewards of triggering capital gains. Since I put my money into fixed income (GICs and bond funds) that only pay interest, I can't take the tax advantages that my neighbors can afford," said Mr. Jones in a frustrated tone.

I said to him, "What if I could invest your money in a bond fund (which you are comfortable holding since it has less risk than an equity fund) and generate capital gains that you can claim against your capital losses? How much would you pay for such a bond fund? Imagine getting 4% to 5% interest next year and not paying tax on it? Well, guess what, a couple of mutual fund companies in Canada have developed bond funds that generate capital gains inside their corporate-class tax funds. This idea only started last year so most investors haven't heard of it. But as more and more Mr. Joneses switch to safer investments, safer doesn't have to mean more tax."

Mr. Jones decided to switch some of his bond fund holdings into corporate-class bond funds (essentially the same type of bonds inside the bond fund he was holding) and recapture capital losses triggered in the last year. When Mr. Jones sells his tax-class bond fund, chances are it will be tax-free.

The next day I had a visit from his neighbors. They asked me how they can keep up with the Joneses.

The best way to prepare for life is to begin to live.
Elbert Hubbard

The whole of life is but a moment of time. It is our duty, therefore to use it, not to misuse it.
Plutarch

Mistake 22
NOT TAKING ADVANTAGE OF TAX-EFFICIENT MONTHLY CASH FLOW TAX STRATEGIES

A Secret Monthly Cash Flow System

Larry from Nanaimo dropped by to ask me how he could start taking income from his mutual funds.

I said, "How would you like to have a majority of it paid to you tax efficiently?"

"Of course, but how can I do that?" Larry answered.

I replied, "Larry, if you're looking for tax-efficient income solutions, here is an idea to think about. Set up a systematic withdrawal program (SWP)."

The concept is simple: You withdraw a specific monthly amount from your mutual fund. Consider it the opposite of dollar cost averaging: A majority of the initial income is a return of your own money or capital, which is tax-efficient. You can state the withdrawal either as a percentage of the fund's value or as a specific monthly amount–say $500 per month. The fund will direct the deposit to your bank account each month, so you don't have to worry about lost mail.

A specific dollar amount, rather than a percentage, is recommended, because the monthly income will not fluctuate. To help protect your money, you should consider withdrawing less than what the fund earns. It will help you keep pace with inflation and possibly increase the income in the future.

In my experience, most investors set up withdrawals of 4% to 6%, although you can set up withdrawals of as much as 9%. (In such cases, we warn clients that they are increasing the risk of eroding the principal.) In an ideal world, Larry will withdraw 6% from a fund that is producing 7% to 8%. That way, the fund will continue to grow over time.

Larry and I chose balanced funds for SWPs, although you can also do it with other kinds of funds. We chose balanced funds because they are highly diversified–with stocks, bonds, Government securities, cash, and sometimes even international securities. A bond fund is unlikely to consistently earn 7% to 8%, and a stock fund is too risky for clients who depend on investment income. Balanced funds form a nice, equitable plan for Larry's retirement income needs.

As an investor looking for income, you probably already know about the stability and reliability that money market funds, GICs, and other fixed income investments can bring to your portfolio; however, the income you earn from these traditional fixed income investments is subject to the highest rate of taxation in Canada. Finally, the mutual funds industry has created a way to generate tax-efficient cash flow for retirees while assets can continue to grow. These are called "tax-class" or "Series T" strategies. (Some companies may have similar names and not all companies offer these tax strategies.)

Some of the benefits of Series T strategies are:

1. High, predictable, and tax-efficient cash flow. Monthly Series T cash flow is targeted at a rate of 5% to 8% per year and is usually paid out monthly on the value of each unit you own, which makes it a highly tax-efficient way for you to meet your regular income goals.

2. Flexibility to customize your cash flow around your specific requirements. Switching between series of the same fund or portfolio is not a taxable disposition. This allows you to fine-tune your cash flow to suit your changing needs. Most fund companies consider switching your investments around as a taxable disposition, which limits your ability to change your investments in the future. Ask your financial advisor whether this is an option for your nonregistered investments.

3. Continue to grow your assets. With a wide range of Series T funds and portfolios from which to choose, you can select a solution that provides you with the tax-deferred cash flow you need and the continued potential for growth of your portfolio.

So how does Series T work? Return of capital (ROC) is the key and allows you to defer 100% of the capital gains tax and enjoy a higher cash flow now.

We all want to minimize the amount of tax we pay on our investments. I'm writing this to tell investors about a strategy that will allow them to save for their retirement outside of their registered plans and still retain the benefits of tax-deferred compound growth—as well as the added bonus of tax-efficient withdrawals. Retirees who should consider this are:
-Those looking for tax-deferred cash flow and some growth on their investments outside RRSPs.
-Those topping up tax brackets with their income and planning capital gains.
-Those looking for cash flow that will not trigger Old-age Securities (OAS) program claw-backs.

Providing Tax-efficient Monthly Cash Flow

Investors today are wondering what they should do about their existing investments in mutual funds—stay invested, change now, or change later.

If you're looking for investment solutions, here are two ideas to think about.

Set up a withdrawal program. You can use those funds for income, or you can reinvest into more conservative investments such as fixed income or bond funds to protect your capital.

Set up a tax-efficient systematic withdrawal program, or "T-SWP." T-SWP investors enjoy a high level of monthly cash flow, from 5% to 8%. They also may have a reduced short-term tax bill.

We did the latter with Gerry, a retiree in Comox, about nine months ago. He had a balanced fund that was not performing well. While he wanted less risk, he didn't want to change all of his investments at one time. We set up a T-SWP that pays Gerry a monthly amount, and we invest monthly into a bond fund to increase the bond holdings in his portfolio. Over time his bond holdings will increase and will make his portfolio more conservative. Gerry will want to take the income in the future, but for now he wants to try to preserve his capital.

The T-SWP works this way. Each month, investors receive a cash distribution of approximately 6% to 8% of the net asset value of the fund over a five-year cycle. These distributions consist primarily of return of capital, which is treated as part of an investor's original investment and therefore is not subject to tax. The tax advantage comes from the fund companies' structures. The capital gains are taxable when units are sold or the original capital invested runs out. The investors have more control—they trigger capital gains instead of the fund company.

If you're looking to make your portfolio more conservative, or for retirement income, it's a good idea to do it over a period of time instead of all at once.

No man is happy who does not think himself so.
Publilius Syrus

If you can DREAM it, you can DO it.
Walt Disney

Mistake 23
OVERLOOKING A POWERFUL ONE-TWO TAX PUNCH IN RETIREMENT

Don't Just Buy a Mutual Fund–Combine Corporate Class and T-SWP

As mentioned in the previous chapter, some companies allow you to set up a T-SWP tax-advantaged withdrawal program and switch between investments without triggering tax. Now you get the best of both worlds, corporate-class and SWP or T-SWP. The final kicker is that any capital gains you have can be given to charity at a zero tax base. That is correct, you can set up a corporate-class fund and generate income from T-SWP, mostly tax-free, and name a charity–with no tax consequences when you die. Wow, what a great concept. It actually works and conforms to the *Income Tax Act*; just ask your accountant and financial professional for details before proceeding. But it is simple–have your cake (corporate-class) and eat it, too (income-tax efficient and free upon death when given to a charity).

Opportunity dances with those who are ready on the dance floor.
H. Jackson Brown, Jr.

Don't wait for extraordinary circumstance to do good; try to use ordinary situations.
Charles Richter

Mistake 24
MISSING PENSION INCOME-SPLITTING OPPORTUNITIES

Learning about the Federal budget every year can save you tax dollars every year. If you are earning income from a pension plan and having tax taken off at source, you may be paying too much tax.

Tim from Coquitlam, a retired fireman, has a pension plan that deducts tax based on the pension he receives. Christine, his spouse, does not have any income. Tim can split as much as 50% of his pension income with Christine this year, lowering his annual income tax bill by as much as 30% on the split portion of his pension plan. Since Tim is having tax withheld by his pension plan at his income bracket and not the combined income bracket, he will be due for a tax refund in April, unless he asks the pension plan to consider lowering the amount of tax taken at source. This would increase Tim and Christine's cash flow today instead of in April. There are no age restrictions, since Christine is younger than Tim. Christine's tax return will show income and Tim's will reduce the income. This may also affect the old-age pension claw-back for taxes on high-income retirees over 65. It may also affect nonrefundable tax credits when they do their tax returns. The pension credit for Tim is available on the first $2,000 of pension income. This will double the credit since Christine will have half of Tim's pension income and will also qualify for the $2,000 pension income credit.

For individuals aged 65 and over the pension splitting applies for benefits from a registered pension plan, RRIF, or registered annuity. If you are under age 65 it applies to benefits from a registered pension plan or certain amounts received as a result of the death of a spouse. Check with your financial advisor, tax professional, and pension office to see if you might increase your cash flow today.

Avoid Excessive Taxation

What will you do with extra income? Mrs. Jones from Qualicum beach emailed me an interesting question. She asked if she should convert some of her RRSPs into a RRIF in order to take advantage of the pension-income credit and to get some tax-free money out of her RRSP. I answered with a question. How old are you?

Mrs. Jones is 68 years old. She could have started taking money out tax-free at age 65; however, she can start this year. Here's how it works. The *Income Tax Act* allows for a $2,000 pension income credit per person per year. To qualify for the credit you need to have pension income excluding Canada Pension Plan and old-age pension. This would be income from a pension plan. If you do not have a pension plan then you can set up income from a RRIF to qualify for the credit. Mrs. Jones transferred enough money from one of her RRSPs to give her the $2,000 per year, tax-free, to which she is entitiled—until she turns 69. If she had started when she was 65, she would have been able to get more tax-free money out of her RRSP.

A retired couple with no pensions can take out $4,000 per year tax-free from their RRSPs, as long as they convert it to RRIFs because it must be RRIF income in order to qualify for the pension-income credit. This will give Mrs. Jones $2,000 more tax-free dollars to spend, so her neighbors will have a tougher time keeping up.

Do what you can, with what you have, where you are.
Theodore Roosevelt

The pessimist sees difficulty in every opportunity. The optimist sees the opportunity in every difficulty.
Winston Churchill

Mistake 25

NOT TAKING BACK YOUR OAS CLAW

You work your whole life and retire at 65. Then, because you worked so hard, the Government keeps the pension that you were promised. It hardly seems fair. How can you stop this?

It may take a little planning. The Old Age Security (OAS) program includes a basic pension, indexed for inflation every January, April, July, and October. The claw-back occurs if your net individual income is above a set threshold (currently $66,335). This figure is also adjusted each year for inflation. For every dollar of income above the threshold, the amount of basic OAS pension reduces by 15 cents. It is clear from my conversations with retirees that many are concerned about this. Here are some simple strategies to help you minimize the claw-back.

1. Defer RRSP income. Eventually, RRSPs must be converted to income. In fact, the latest you can defer a RRSP is December 31 of the year in which you turn 71 and then take the minimum withdrawal each year to minimize your net income.

2. If you have a younger spouse, use his or her age for RRIF planning to calculate the minimum RRIF income. It will lower your income.

3. Tax-efficient income on nonregistered RSP investments. When it comes to investment income from nonregistered investments, different types of income are taxed differently. Interest income from GICs and term deposits are taxed at a high rate. Dividend income and capital gains enjoy a much lower tax rate.

4. Use part of your nonregistered funds to purchase an annuity to provide an income stream. From a tax perspective, only a portion

of each payment is taxable because a portion of each payment is considered a return of capital and is, therefore, tax-free.

5. If you are able to split your income with your spouse, you may be able to reduce your net income. Some examples include CPP splitting, investment income, and payments from corporations.

6. Final RRSP contribution. Up until and including age 71, if you have unused RRSP deduction room, make a final RRSP contribution.

7. Finally, for couples, the new pension-splitting rules can help reduce or eliminate the claw-back. Some couples who are not married may consider the advantages of filing together if they have been living together for awhile.

Check to see whether a portion of your OAS is being clawed back and plan to take it back for yourself.

When written in Chinese, the word "crisis" is composed of two characters—one represents danger, and the other represents opportunity.
John F. Kennedy

The great accomplishments of man have resulted from the transmission of ideas and enthusiasm.
Thomas J. Watson, Sr.

Mistake 26
THE TEN BIGGEST RRSP MISTAKES

I have seen the rise and fall of RRSP programming. I saw investors pour money into RRSPs trying to maximize every tax deduction and save for retirement. Today investors are wondering whether it is still a good idea. Remember, it is a tax deduction today, not at retirement. Here are some of the mistakes I have seen.

First, procrastination–putting it off each year and then planning to really save at a later date. The key factor as an investor is time and the compounding growth. Investing a small amount earlier may help you retire earlier.

Second, not knowing the real cost of your retirement. In retirement planning, don't ask yourself when you want to retire but how much you need each month during your retirement. Keep that number in your head as your key retirement goal. If you have enough to meet your plans, then you are in control and can say when you will retire.

Third, not understanding what risk really means. The greatest risk to investments, about which few people are aware, is inflation. Over time, inflation erodes returns, in turn reducing your future buying power. To keep ahead, your money has to work for you and your portfolio returns need to keep ahead of inflation.

Fourth, inadequate diversification. Diversify your portfolio by asset class, geography, and style of investments. Do you have all your equity investments in Canada? Can you name three or four holdings inside your RRSP right now? Are you comfortable with these holdings? Ask yourself these three tough questions.

Fifth, buying mutual funds based on last year's performance. Hey, anyone can pick a five-star fund; that's why they rate funds, so everyone can pick them. Find a consistent performer and management style over the long term, say five years. Be skeptical of spectacular performance results from small funds. High single-year numbers should raise caution flags. Remember, as investors we are looking for bargains.

Sixth, staying too long with losing investments. I know it is difficult to change, but you can ask for help. Talk to an advisor who can help you change what isn't working. One phone call may give your portfolio new life.

Seventh, missing income-splitting opportunities by not purchasing spousal RRSPs. Although the current Government rules allow for income splitting in retirement, the rules may not apply to you or may change again.

Eighth, not naming a beneficiary. Your spouse can receive your RRSP tax-free and you can also name a charity (with certain provisions) as a beneficiary.

Ninth, disorganization, having statements all over the place and missing maturities and holdings. Ask your advisor to help consolidate and get organized.

Tenth, not realizing how easy it is to transfer RRSPs from one institution to another. Most financial institutions can hold assets of any kind and transferring is relatively easy and tax-free.

Good luck avoiding making RRSP mistakes.

Here's Relief for April 30

Does April 30 drain you? It's the annual income tax filing deadline. If you would like to effortlessly put money back into your life before the deadline, here are some solutions for you.

Figure out if you are going to owe money this year. If the answer is yes, consider these possibilities. Look towards tax deductions. Now that the year is over, the final remaining tax deduction is your RRSP. That's right. We are all too busy in December and would rather think of Santa Claus than the Grinches in Ottawa. But there is still time. You have until March 1 to make a RRSP contribution. The common question is how much. A simple rule of thumb is 10% to 15% of your gross income. "Right. Grant, I can't afford that." Well then, do the next best thing, put in what you can afford and consider a RRSP loan. If you're getting money back, a loan makes complete sense. Borrow the money now, get it back in April, and pay off the loan. Simple math and easy to do, unless of course you enjoy sending cheques to the Government.

The next argument is, "I heard RRSPs aren't that great anymore." Now I'll stop that argument with, "If I could guarantee you 25% to 40% return on your money immediately, would you invest? Where else can you invest and do that?"

A RRSP provides you with a tax deduction for this coming April; and while the money grows, it's tax-sheltered. When you retire, you only pay tax on what you take out; and you're in control of that until you are 71, when you have to take out a certain amount each year.

Only in Canada, eh? Pity. Other counties don't have a generous RRSP program, yet only 5% of Canadians maximize their RRSPs every year. Go ahead, be a skeptic, pay the Government. After all, it's only money.

Is Your RRSP Locked In?

Another common error is misunderstanding locked-in RRSPs. Individuals with money in locked-in RRSPs usually find themselves waiting too long to use the money and finding out that they cannot take out from the plan as much as they expected. If you have money in a locked-in RRSP, there are a few strategies you can use to get the maximum amount of money out earlier. Before you transfer your locked-in RRSP to a LIF, LIRA, or LRIF, check which will pay out the most over your lifetime. Each Provincial pension plan has different rules and Federal pensions are also distinct.

As early as possible, plan to take out the annual maximum. This is 55 years of age, if the funds are from a BC pension plan. If the funds are from another province, you may take it out earlier;

for example, the age in Alberta is 50. Once you transfer to a LIF or LRIF plan to take out the maximum available each year, Provincial pension legislation calculates a maximum amount that can be withdrawn. If the maximum is not withdrawn, it continues to be locked in. All withdrawals are included in income for the year and are subject to tax. However, if you are still working, you can withdraw the maximum from your locked-in RRSP and contribute those funds into a regular RRSP, therefore not attracting any tax and unlocking funds each year. This works for anyone under age 70.

Once the money is in a RRSP, you can withdraw any amount at any time. This gradually unlocks your money over time and you can do this each year.

If you have a small locked-in plan, you can transfer it to a regular RRSP and take it out any time. The definition of "small plan" changes and varies by province, but it is targeted for plans approximately $16,400 and less. Keeping up with each provincial change is challenging, but ask your sponsoring plan administrator or financial professional. Plan to unlock as much as possible as soon as possible, and knowing how can enhance your retirement income flexibility. Visit the provincial Web sites for the latest updates and tax changes.

Some men go through a forest and see no firewood.
English Proverb

It is no disgrace to start all over. It is usually an opportunity.
George Matthew Adams

Mistake 27
FAILING TO MAXIMIZE YOUR RRIF

What happens when you turn 71? You must collapse your RSP into an approved retirement income option by the end of the calendar year in which you turn 71. It's important to remember that if you do not take action, the financial institution that holds your RSP will be required to collapse it for you according to Canada Revenue Agency (CRA) regulations. You would be taxed on the full amount in a single year.

How do you get your money out of a RRSP? Recently I did a presentation, to a group of retirees, on registered retirement income funds (RRIFs). We discussed the general rules of RRIFs, such as the age which you must turn your RRSPs into RRIFs (71). Your withdrawal amounts are based on a formula, which you can find at <www.retireware.com>.

If you are 70 years old, the minimum you must withdraw per year is 5% of the value of the plan at the beginning of the year. In the group presentation, we discussed three RRIF strategies based on three different types of investors.

First there's Marcus, who has enough retirement income and is worried about capital preservation and CPP claw-back. He decides to take the minimum payment at the end of the year and base the payments on his younger wife's age so the minimum payment is lower. He is looking for less income from his RRIF.

Next is Brendan, who doesn't really need a lot more income but enjoys the additional income his RRIF can provide. He wants to try to preserve capital but doesn't mind it slowly declining over time to keep up with inflation, since he has other investments on which to fall back. He withdraws the minimum for a number of years. At age 70 his withdrawal is 5% of the value of his plan and at age 71 it increases to 7.38% of the value of the plan. He knows that the minimum increases over time and that if he is not earning the minimum he will be slowly reducing his capital. He is prepared to do that for his retirement plan, and knows his capital will slowly decline. He then considers to plan transferring the funds to an annuity when he is around 80 to give him a comfortable income for life.

Finally there's Todd. He doesn't mind his RRIF depleting over time, he doesn't have any major tax concerns, and he isn't worried about preserving his capital for his estate. He sets up a withdrawal of 1% per month, 12% per year. He wants the additional income now and is prepared to deplete his RRIF funds. Todd is a more aggressive investor and doesn't mind fluctuations in the value of his portfolio.

Each of the three investors has different paths to choose when it comes to getting their money out of their RRIF.

Which of these Mistakes are You Making with Your RRIF?

1. Not deferring payment. For investors who do not need additional income, defer the payment until the end of the year so your money is tax-sheltered as long as possible.

2. Not basing income on the younger spouse. If you have a younger spouse, base the payments on his or her age. This gives you more time to defer income if needed, especially if your spouse is several years younger.

3. Not designating a beneficiary. For couples, it is best to name your spouse, since it is a tax-free rollover upon death of one spouse. It is also free of probate and does not form part of the estate. For single seniors who want to bequeath to their children, naming the estate can cause delays such as probate, probate fees, and withholding of tax. If you name the children, the financial institution pays out directly to the beneficiaries and the estate or executor is responsible for paying the tax. This may also cause another problem, if there is not enough in the estate and the

executor is an outsider who may have to go back to the children and collect the tax. Proper planning is crucial for single seniors with RRIFs.

4. Not taking advantage of unused contribution room. Maximize RRSPs before you turn 70 or roll them all into RRIFs. Unused RRSP contributions, even at the age of 69, can help save thousands of tax dollars this year.

5. Too-risky investments. Hey, this is your retirement income. A stock portfolio is not designed for retirement income. Look at income-generating investments for safety and security. Plan on spending it, not growing it. That's what you saved the money for in the first place, isn't it?

Tips to Help Maximize Returns in Your RIF

Make sure your investor profile hasn't changed since you retired.

Speak to your financial advisor about your asset allocation to ensure you have the right asset mix.

Ask your financial advisor about consolidating your registered and nonregistered investments into just two accounts so that you can more easily manage your asset mix and income withdrawal.

If you need to use your capital, in most instances it's advisable to use your nonregistered assets first. Because your registered investments are tax-sheltered, it makes sense to leave them intact for as long as possible.

If you need to take income from your RIF, decide how often you'll need it—monthly, quarterly, semi-annually, or annually. If you're only withdrawing the annual minimum payment (AMP), withdraw it at the end of the year so that you enjoy the greatest tax-sheltered growth.

If you have a younger spouse, use his or her age to calculate the AMP. This will allow you to withdraw less.

Laddering (proportioning investment dollars evenly across bonds or GICs of differing maturities) is an effective way to make sure all your money doesn't come due at once when interest rates may be very low.

If you find you don't need as much money as you thought you would, ask your advisor about changing the payment schedule to lower amounts or less frequency. Otherwise you'll be paying tax on money you don't need.

Depending on your investment time horizon, personal tolerance for risk, investment knowledge, and other factors that make up your investor profile, it could be important to have some growth in the form of stocks and equity funds, or dividend income funds, in your RIF. This strategy may be right for you to help protect against inflation and ensure that a portion of your capital continues to appreciate.

Be diversified—it's just as important now as it was before you retired. When possible, keep your interest income investments in your RIF, where they can accumulate in a tax-deferred account; and keep your growth and dividend-paying investments outside your RIF—capital gains and dividends are taxed at a lower rate.

Finally (this may go without saying), don't gamble with your retirement investments. Look at options to protect your investments and take a lifetime perspective.

You can't build a reputation on what you're going to do.
Henry Ford

I always tried to turn every disaster into an opportunity.
John D. Rockefeller, Jr.

Mistake 28
NOT EXPLORING WAYS OF SAVING THOUSANDS OF DOLLARS THROUGH TAX REDUCTION

Do-it-yourself Tax Returns

I have seen too many seniors try to cheap out on tax advice. If the cost of a professional is too high, stop complaining about high taxes–because you are not even exploring the possibility of savings.

Retiring Allowances

Yesterday, Alex called from Nanaimo with great news, he's finally retiring. He's receiving a retiring allowance from his employer and wants some help in tax planning. A retiring allowance is money received on or after retirement in recognition of long service. It can include payments for unused sick leave credits and/or severance packages and payouts. For tax planning, having funds designated as a retiring allowance regardless of your age qualifies for additional RRSP contribution amounts and does not affect your current contribution amounts. Companies can also offer the payout over two or more years so they don't have to come up with the funds right away; then the employee can plan to take income over a few years to spread out any possible tax liability.

Alex began working with his company in 1983 and is about to receive $40,000 as termination pay, $2,500 for unused sick leave, and $1,500 for vacation pay. His retiring allowance is calculated as $42,500. He wants to know the best way to shelter the payout from a big tax hit. He was allowed to contribute to a RRSP in a combination of $2,000 per year before 1996 and an additional $1,500 per year of service before 1989. In Alex's case he can transfer $35,000, tax-free, to a RRSP, plus any unused contribution room he has carried forward. His carry-forward was $9,000, so we were able to transfer the entire retiring allowance, tax-free, to his

RRSP. If Alex wants to take it out one day after the transfer he can. He can now decide when to trigger the tax and how much.

Severance Strategies

Losing a job raises a lot of concerns, not to mention tax planning concerns. Will from Port Alberni came in the other day and asked me for some help on his company severance package. First, we talked about negotiating to take his severance over two years to spread out the tax liability. Second, we made sure that he topped up his unused RRSP contributions. Severance income can often be offset with RRSP rollover based on eligible service. Using remaining severance payments to top up previously unused RRSP room can also be effective, especially over several years. Third, we discussed the possibility of withdrawing from RRSPs if necessary. When cash flow falls short of needs, withdraw RRSP accumulations in a lower-income year. Fourth, we took into account all the possible refundable tax credits to which he is entitled and offset income taxes payable with these amounts, even if that means projecting taxes forward a couple of years. This gives him a true net tax cost that relates to his cash flow timing. It can sometimes be better to forego some tax credits available in the future in order to minimize taxes payable today. We also looked at making use of labor-sponsored tax credits. Since Will doesn't mind higher-risk investments, he is interested in getting his tax bill down this year.

The final part of his planning came down to his pension plan. He had the option of transferring his pension plan to a locked-in RRSP or keeping it with his former employer. His is a strong, indexed pension; so this decision was relatively easy. It is difficult to beat an indexed pension plan, especially a strong one. We decided it was best to leave it with his employer. He'll thank me in years to come, when his pension cheque increases each year. Will now has less tax worry when it comes to his severance.

There are costs and risks to a program of action, but they are far less than the long-range risks and costs of comfortable inaction.
John F. Kennedy

A wise man will make more opportunities than he finds.
Francis Bacon

Mistake 29
NOT BUYING BACK YOUR PENSION

A common question among professionals, such as teachers
or Provincial employees, is whether they should buy back
their pensions. Take the case of Jason and Carol Anne.
One is a teacher and the other works for the Federal
Government. Both have strong pension plans but Carol
Anne has the ability to buy back five years of hers. The
cost is more than $30,000. She wonders if she is better off
investing the money into a RRSP. At 48 years of age, the
answer is simple. Carol Anne is better off buying back
the pension. The simple reason is that her pension plan is
indexed. This means that when she retires, her pension plan
payments will increase every year for the rest of her life.
This can be a significant gain and can offset inflationary costs
during retirement. Her investments would have to provide a
reasonable rate of return, like her pension plan, and increase
every year during retirement in order for this to be the more
attractive option. When you crunch the numbers, in most
cases it is difficult to beat an indexed pension.

Carol Anne's next question is where she should come up
with the money she needs to buy back the pension. She has
$15,000 cash, should she borrow the rest? I suggest we do a
tax-free transfer from her existing RRSP, which has $50,000
in it. She can use $30,000 from her RRSP, keep the $15,000
cash, and not worry about borrowing costs or payments;
or she can use part cash and part RRSP. It does depend on
her income and her current tax situation. After some simple
income tax planning, she decides to use $20,000 of her RRSP
and $10,000 cash to buy back her pension. The remaining

$5,000 cash is retained as emergency funds, providing a feeling of comfort. Now Carol Anne and Jason will have a more secure retirement.

What you do speaks so loud that I cannot hear what you say.
Ralph Waldo Emerson

Leadership is practiced not so much in words as in attitude and in actions.
Harold S. Geneen

Mistake 30
NOT CUTTING SENIORS' TAX WITH PRESCRIBED ANNUITIES

If you're more than 65 years of age and looking for a low-risk way to reduce taxes on retirement income while boosting your monthly cash flow, you might want to consider prescribed annuities. The word "annuity" can scare off a lot of people because in the past most annuities died with the person who set them up. Today, however, insurance companies hungry for retirees' business offer a range of flexible annuities, some having guarantees for beneficiaries for ten and fifteen years of payments.

The plan is simple. You lock away a fixed amount of money in return for income for life. You can set up individual or joint annuities with your spouse. You set a guaranteed beneficiary payment period, say five or ten years from the start date of the annuity, for after your death. The key here though, often overlooked, is taxation. If you're getting clawed-back old age pension and you see your income diminish and your quarterly income tax installment bill rising, consider an annuity for part of your income. The annuity reduces the amount of taxes payable because it "amortizes the investment income over the life of the annuity."

If your spouse is in a high tax bracket and generates a lot of interest income, annuities can reduce the tax bill. Most professionals recommend annuities, but usually to a maximum of 25% of your investment portfolio. The ideal investor is usually past the age of 70 and is paying tax installments quarterly or has large income tax deductions from retirement income.

But not all investors are older than 70. Some annuities work well with people in their 60s, who can sometimes qualify for insured annuities, which guarantee the principal amount tax-free to beneficiaries upon death. This is done by purchasing a life insurance policy. Insurance companies also allow you to purchase insurance on a smaller amount of the principal. Talk to your financial professional to see if annuities might help boost your income and reduce your tax bill.

Why would Dave, a 72-year-old retiree from Qualicum, switch his RRIF to an annuity? Retirement income planning tells us that the primary aim of most of our investing is to provide income for when we can no longer earn it. To maximize this future income we try to maximize the growth of our investments while minimizing any risks. Dave looked for a secure, stable income that he cannot outlive; but when he switched from accumulating investments to drawing on them he discovered that the income from most is both erratic and temporary. Interest rates and dividend levels change; GICs and bonds mature; and we are forced to seek other investments.

For Dave, a joint life annuity will address his and his wife's income needs for as long as either of them are alive, which is just one of the reasons Dave switched. A few of the others are capital erosion, level income, mortality, simplification, insurance, and permanence. Here is Dave's thinking behind each reason.

Capital erosion–Last year Dave's RRIF earnings averaged only 5.69% while the mandatory minimum withdrawal was 7.38%. As the payout was higher than the profit, the difference had to come from capital. Also, as the minimum withdrawal rate keeps increasing, until it levels out at 20%, the capital erosion will keep increasing. The capital will eventually be completely exhausted, eaten up in its final years by the fees of the RRIF trustee.

Level income–Dave wanted a level monthly income for life.

Mortality–Dave or his wife can easily outlive a level RRIF income, but they can't outlive the income from a joint life annuity.

Simplification–Accumulating investments accumulate paper. There's a great quantity of data about them–certificates, statements, records, etc.–and it is a chore just to keep track of them all.

Insurance–The purpose of most life insurance is to provide a lifelong income for one's widow. A joint life annuity does exactly that.

Permanence–A life annuity is permanent.

There are a lot of seniors like Dave who haven't thought of the advantages that an annuity has over a RRIF. Are you one?

Nowadays some people expect the door of opportunity to be opened with a remote control.
M. Charles Wheeler

If you can give your son or daughter only one gift, let it be enthusiasm.
Bruce Barton

Mistake 31
NOT EXPLORING INSURANCE TAX SHELTERS

The life insurance industry is a tax haven. It was a way of sheltering money from taxation long before RRSPs came into existence and is a strategy used by the wealthy. It is essentially a plan that allows you to deposit money into a life insurance contract and to shelter all of the growth of the investment from income tax. Canada Revenue Agency allows insurance companies to issue policies and maintain their tax shelter status under certain conditions. These insurance plans are considered exempt under Sections 12.2 and 148 of the *Income Tax Act.* You must pay for a minimum amount of life insurance to keep the plan tax-exempt. The life insurance industry has developed these tax-exempt products for years and can help you meet several objectives.

First, regardless of the amount that you have sheltered from tax, the entire amount of the cash and/or the death benefit (depending on the type of contract) is paid tax-free and probate-free upon death. It is a great way to pass on wealth to the next generation tax-free. Second, it allows you to grow and protect your wealth inside a tax-free insurance contract. While your account grows there is no taxation, and you can choose from a wide range of investment options. Third, the life insurance contract can provide you with tax-efficient retirement income and, if structured properly, can provide you with tax-free retirement income. Under a special arrangement, you can leverage your investments inside the plan with a bank. The leverage is only repayable upon death and is guaranteed by the life insurance proceeds.

Most Canadian chartered accounting firms have published
materials promoting the tax-advantaged benefits of insurance tax
shelters. Ask your financial advisor or tax professional whether
an insurance tax shelter can work for you and your family.

*Accept yourself as you are. Otherwise you will never see opportunity. You will not
feel free to move toward it; you will feel you are not deserving.*
Maxwell Maltz

Create a definite plan for carrying out your desire and begin at once, whether you are ready or not, to put this plan into action.
Napoleon Hill

Mistake 32
EARNING INTEREST INCOME INSIDE YOUR RRSP/RRIF INSTEAD OF OUTSIDE

Are you one of those investors who doesn't mind risk inside your registered plan, RRSP, or RRIF but want the money that you have outside of your RRSP to be safe and liquid? Several retirees I have seen have made this common mistake. They are generating capital gains income inside their tax-sheltered plan and interest income, fully taxable, each year outside their tax-sheltered plan. If the investments were switched—meaning no additional risk, just different positioning—it would save taxes today and every year in your retirement. Look at making a simple switch and consider swapping assets if you're in this situation. Talk to your advisor and or tax professional before proceeding.

Here is another tax-saving income idea to consider. Set up a withdrawal program. You can use those funds for income or you can reinvest that income into more conservative investments, such as fixed income or bond funds, to protect your capital. How about a tax-efficient A-SWP? A-SWP investors enjoy a high level of monthly cash flow and, perhaps, a reduced tax bill in the short term. We did this with Keith, a retiree in Comox. He had a balanced fund that was not performing well. While he wanted less risk, he didn't want to change all of his investments at this time. We set up a tax-advantaged A-SWP that pays Keith monthly, and we invest monthly into a bond fund to increase the bond holdings in his portfolio. Over time his bond holdings will increase and make his portfolio more conservative. Keith will want to take the income in the future, but for now he wants to try to preserve his capital in his retirement.

See Mistake 22, "Not Taking Advantage of Tax-efficient Monthly Cash Flow Tax Strategies."

If you're looking for ways to make your portfolio more conservative, or for retirement income, here is one idea: Do it over a period of time instead of all at once.

If God only gave me a clear sign; like making a large deposit in my name at a Swiss bank.
Woody Allen

Chapter 3

REDUCE

MINIMIZE INCOME TAX SO YOU
CAN HAVE MORE CASH FLOW
TO ENJOY SUCH THINGS AS
TRAVEL, HOME DECORATING, OR
CHARITABLE PURSUITS

GRANT HICKS

Commitment leads to action. Action brings your dream closer.
Marcia Wieder

Mistake 33
COMMON MISTAKES IN WEALTH TRANSFERS

Estate planning is just like planning a trip: Leave proper instructions, including keys, to people you trust. If you have been an executor, you know the kind of patience you need in dealing with an estate. Rarely is it easy; and when it is, something usually gets missed. Leaving an estate to family members can cause more problems than you might think. Family disputes can be avoided with careful, well-thought-out planning.

The first step is communication. I usually recommend that parents discuss with their children their general intentions–not specific dollar amounts. Another great idea I picked up along the way is to create an estate binder, a file containing relevant documents for the executor. This would include copies of important documents such as the will, insurance policies, property titles, investments and banking info. Include important contact information for any tax, legal, financial, and insurance advisors.

Your executor will lose sleep if you have no will or if it cannot be easily located. Hey, make it simple to find if you have one. What if your family does not know it is in the safety deposit box?

Also a problem is when there are no declarations in the will in regard to gifts. If you plan to leave gifts, make sure all are clearly spelled out in your will.

Make the most of your final tax return. Assets that are jointly owned with children do not form part of the estate. If there are assets being bequeathed, is that done in equal proportion for each of the children? Or did one child receive an additional part outside the will as a joint account holder?

Lack of records or disorganized records is a common problem for executors and family members. To simplify, you could make an up-to-date statement of all investments with a note such as, "These records are up to date as of June, 2009; you do not have to search every bank in Canada to find out where our money is." Communication and a bit of record keeping may help you and or your executors sleep better.

Never confuse motion with action.
Benjamin Franklin

Just Do It!
Nike Running Shoes Advertisement

Mistake 34

THE $100,000 MISTAKE

I get calls every week from investors wanting to know the best place to invest money. It's a reasonable question, but I often find that the investor is focused on the wrong part of his or her financial situation. Does it really matter if an investor can get a 12% return if the plan gets ignored and the Government gets an unnecessary $100,000 in taxes? Wouldn't it make more sense for an investor to focus on the best way to save that $100,000 than to focus on how to invest $50,000 to earn another $3,000 per year? The answer is obvious, but it's often not what happens. Why? Most investors incorrectly believe that estate planning is about giving money away and losing control of their assets.

If you listen to many professionals, it sounds like estate planning is about relinquishing control of your assets. In fact, estate planning is about maintaining control of your assets. If you don't like how the Government spends your money, estate planning will redirect how your money is spent, based on your desires.

Therefore, estate planning is about taking maximum control of your money and directing it the way you desire, not the way the Government or another other family member desires. Investors also fail to do estate planning because of just plain ignorance or gaps in their knowledge. Some investors still think that if they have a trust, they'll pay no estate taxes. This is a widely held misconception. Other investors hate talking about estate planning because they'll have to confront mortality. And as mentioned before, some investors think that estate planning means giving money away.

In fact, good estate planning starts with making sure you have ample resources for yourself. Only when that is ascertained can estate planning begin. Estate planning boils down to one simple issue–do you want to have control of your money?

How do you start? Completing a questionnaire (most lawyers and retirement and estate planning professionals use one when completing a will) will help you focus on your goals, assets, and desires. The questionnaire is followed up with an interview to help translate the answers into specific desires. Then you can work on determining ways to achieve what you want to have happen. This avoids the mistake that many make–jumping right into the tools (trusts, gifting, insurance) only to learn later that the tools don't work as desired.

If you really want to make a big difference in your financial picture, it may make more sense to focus on estate planning than on how to get a higher percentage on your investments.

Go for it now. The future is promised to no one.
Wayne Dyer

You will never plough a field if you only turn it over in your mind.
Irish Proverb

Mistake 35
NOT BEING AWARE OF THE RISKS IN JOINT ACCOUNTS

Did you hear the story of the retiree who had his accounts cleaned out by his son? It can easily happen if you put your investments and bank accounts in joint accounts. If you become mentally incapacitated, your children can take the money, leaving you broke at a time you need help. Most couples set up joint investment accounts for banking, investing, real estate, and motor vehicle purchases. But when a spouse dies, joint accounting can become more complicated.

There are several benefits for joint accounts, including probate-free transfer upon death, income splitting for spouses, and ease of estate administration. But the pitfalls can be greater.

The primary risk is loss of control. Some accounts require both signatures. If your children live across the country and your investment matures or you need funds to take a trip, you may need their signatures and consent. Another problem is that joint accounts may become part of creditor proceedings if one of the joint account holders declares bankruptcy. Even worse, a joint account can be named as an asset in a marriage or common-law relationship breakdown and may be subject to division. If you have more than one child, the accounts that have only one child as joint account holder can cause family disputes, increasing the costs. Another common problem is taxation. If you put your children on as joint owners of your principal residence, they may lose that principal-residence exemption and create a potential capital gain. Also it may eliminate qualification for the first-time home buyers' program. With proper planning and strategies, probate fees can be reduced or eliminated.

Creating joint accounts to simplify probate fees and estate planning should be carefully thought out. Consider designating your children as beneficiaries through investing with life insurance companies, and consult your financial advisor.

Organized crime in America takes in over forty billion dollars a year and spends very little on office supplies.
Woody Allen

Chapter 4

_____

PROTECT

_____

ASSET-PROTECTION STRATEGIES
SO YOU ARE FREE TO SPEND ON
YOURSELF AND YOUR FAMILY

GRANT HICKS

The great end of life is not knowledge but action.
Thomas H. Huxley

Mistake 36
NOT BEING PREPARED

What if you died today? Thinking about it seems odd, but we all want to have peace of mind about the answer to that question. When answering from a financial perspective, it's natural to want to do the best you can with the finances you have.

Dean's Estate Planning

In the last few years, it has been challenging to get people to spend their money if they are truly savers. Recently I sat down with Dean, a single senior who wanted estate planning advice. He is in his 70s and living in Qualicum. If he doesn't spend all his money, he wants to leave it to his two children. His home, his RRIFs, and his investments are worth about $400,000. Dean has named his children as beneficiaries of his RRIF.

I encouraged him get control of the money by taking more of it out of the RRIF, so he can spend and enjoy it and pay tax as he goes instead of losing almost half when he dies. The money outside his RRSPs is invested in segregated funds. The estate advantage is that he can invest in dividend income funds and generate dividends and capital gains. These funds might pay him more but will not tax him more, and 100% of his capital will be guaranteed to his children if he dies regardless of market conditions. This strategy also bypasses probate, so the payout is immediate.

Dean asked if he should add his children's names as joint owners of his home. I mentioned that they would be responsible for capital gains when the house is sold, since it is not their principal residence. We switched back to his name a GIC that had been jointly held with his boys and invested it into an insurance-

company GIC with the boys as beneficiaries. Finally a will
and power of attorney needed to be set up outlining his wishes
if becomes ill or incapable of making financial decisions. We
referred him to a lawyer or notary public to get the proper legal
advice. Dean left that day with the peace of mind knowing the
answer to the question, "What happens when I die?"

Success seems to be connected to action. Successful people keep moving. They make mistakes, but they don't quit.
Conrad Hilton

If you doubt you can accomplish something, then you can't accomplish it. You have to have confidence in your ability, and then be tough enough to follow through.
Rosalyn Carter

Mistake 37
SECOND MARRIAGE MISTAKES

Let me tell you a secret about estate planning. One day last month, Mick and Tracy walked into my office to discuss estate planning. Mick introduced me to his second wife and joked about the challenges in joining two different families. He said, "When I die, I want to leave enough for my children and everything else to my wife."

Sounds simple. He has a will so everything is set out in the will, right? Most of Mick's assets are jointly owned with Tracy. The home, as well as investments yielding approximately $300,000, will pass outside the will to Tracy. His RRIF, worth about $200,000, names Tracy as beneficiary since it will pass to her tax-free. Even Mick's vehicle is jointly owned with Tracy.

"So, what's left for your children?" I said.

After the dead silence, Mick looked at me and said, "Wow, I never thought of it that way. How do I make sure Tracy will give anything to my children when I die?"

"Tracy's will says everything goes to her children. So if you both die in an accident tomorrow, most of your estate will go to Tracy's children."

Estate planning gets very tricky with second marriages, especially amongst seniors who may have children and grandchildren on both sides. While the will may give you guidance, joint accounts or accounts set up with beneficiary designations will not pass through the will. Mick has to be more specific in his intentions and do some careful planning with his lawyer and accountant or financial advisor; not only about the tax implications but also about the best way to distribute his investments when he dies (as well as when Tracy dies).

The secret of estate planning is to figure out not only how to distribute the funds, but also how to prepare for the challenges faced by those left behind.

Financial Tips for Second Marriages

According to Statistics Canada, remarriage is very common but becoming less so because of the trend towards living together without marriage. About 75% and 65%, respectively, of divorced men and women remarry. In today's world, the same joint-ownership rules may apply both to marriages and to common-law relationships.

Let's look at Fred and Wilma, who were both married previously. Fred was revising his will and wanted to make sure that some money went to his two adult children. In his will, he stipulated that Wilma would get 50% of the estate and his two kids would get 25% each. The problem was that he and Wilma owned the home as "joint tenants." In addition, they had joint bank accounts and joint investment accounts. The way his assets were titled–jointly, with rights of survivorship–the house, the bank account, and the investments would all go to Wilma. The kids would get a percentage of whatever was outside of these investments; in this case, next to nothing.

There are two ways of owning property. The more common is "joint tenancy" with rights of survivorship. Essentially, when property is held jointly the surviving joint owner becomes the owner of the entire property. The property bypasses probate, bypasses the will, and is not part of the estate. Less common is "tenants in common" where each only owns a portion of the property. Upon death, their portion forms part of their estate. In the case of Fred, he may have been better off owning the house as tenants in common with Wilma, to ensure that his kids would get a portion of his property.

RRSP/RRIF Beneficiary Designation

If you name a beneficiary other than your spouse, you must understand the tax consequences. Not only will the RRSP/RRIF be taxable, it will also be taxable to the estate. The estate is responsible for filing the final return.

Betty was widowed and living common-law with her new partner, Barney. Betty wanted to make sure that her daughter Christine got something so she designated her as the beneficiary for her RRSPs. When Betty passed away, Christine got the RRSPs but the estate was responsible for the tax on the RRSPs. Barney and Christine wound up getting into a battle over who would have to pay the tax on the RRSPs. Be careful when listing someone other than a spouse as the beneficiary for a RRSP. As you can see, estate planning for second marriages requires some detailed thought and planning. Don't assume everything will work out. Take the time to plan ahead and seek advice. Rules may also vary from province to province.

Character isn't inherited. One builds it daily by the way one thinks and acts, thought by thought, action by action.
Helen Gahagan Douglas

We can no more afford to spend major time on minor things than we can to spend minor time on major things.
Jim Rohn

Mistake 38
THINKING THAT ESTATE PLANNING IS ABOUT DYING

Talking about estate planning can be as exciting as watching paint dry. But it doesn't have to be all about dying. Here are four reasons why you should consider estate planning.

1. You want to pay less income tax today. Each time you withdraw from your retirement plan, you pay tax. There are a couple of ways to potentially reduce the tax bite. First, fill up the "lower tax brackets." If you postpone, the tax bracket may be higher. This is evident in RRSPs and RRIFs in Canada. A withdrawal at 22% is better than a lump sum at 40% plus.

2. You want to be in control of your retirement money. Therefore, make sure you have the documents that give you control. These would include a will, power of attorney, and possibly a health care directive.

3. You may want to rid yourself of "time-consuming" assets, such as rental real estate, small businesses, or corporations. Typically, these assets are never sold because the owners don't want to pay the capital gains tax. The tax has to be paid, but there are ways to defer it. Discuss strategies with your financial or tax advisor.

4. You want to reduce liability. Retirees sometimes confuse ownership with control. You can give up ownership yet maintain control. For example, you can transfer assets into a trust. You can transfer assets and invest them into an insurance company and have different owners or annuitants and beneficiaries. Segregated funds are used in estate planning

to name children as successor annuitants or beneficiaries while maintaining control over the investment today.

Strategies like these can work well with second marriages. Notice that the payoff is usually for Mom and Dad and not necessarily for the children. If you want more from your money today, then consider learning how an estate plan benefits you and your family.

Will a Large Inheritance cause Problems?

At a conference, I listened to a few interesting stories by Michael Alexander. As the author of the best-selling book *How to Inherit Money: A Guide to Making Good Financial Decisions After Losing Someone You Love,* Michael shared real-life examples, including his own, of people inheriting a lot of money. Over the next 30 years, baby boomers are expected to inherit close to 10 trillion dollars from their parents. As a financial professional, Michael asks, "What questions do you ask people during estate planning?"

He suggested asking, at the planning stage, whether a large sum of money will cause family problems. If you bequeath, without any direction, a large lump sum to a child who is not responsible with money, serious problems can arise for your family. Instead of leaving a legacy, you leave a problem. If you have a child that is disabled or handicapped, will this change their situation? Think what your children would do if they suddenly came into hundreds of thousands of dollars today. What exactly would they do? Michael talked about people inheriting millions and going through it faster than you read this article. Bad investments, lending out money to friends and family, and other examples of irresponsibility are just a few of the many potential problems.

Michael also talked about investing a large inheritance. He suggested parking the money in a short-term account, such as a money market investment or GIC, for six months to one year. Your life dramatically changes when you lose a loved one; turning around and making long-term decisions is difficult at an emotional time like this.

It's also a good idea to discuss your estate plan with your children, without getting into specific figures, so they are aware of and understand your plan. That way, everyone can sleep at night knowing you intend to leave a legacy, not a problem.

Strategies for Eliminating Probate Fees

Sometimes there can be a long list of fees on your estate before your beneficiary gets the money–probate fees, debt repayment, administration expenses and funeral costs, income tax, and capital gains tax. How can you make it simpler? Consider the story of Paul in Victoria, who had an estate of almost a million dollars; but after all fees and expenses and two years, his only son received less than $500,000. Most of his money was in a RRIF and the estate was the beneficiary. He had capital gains tax, income tax, and probate fees. A few simple ideas could have saved a lot of time and expense.

First, proceeds from investments having named beneficiaries bypass probate, legal, and administration fees and are not a matter of public record. He could have named his son beneficiary on his RRIF and his investments, if they were with a life insurance company. The funds would have been paid out within two weeks of Paul's death.

The estate fee in British Columbia, on the portion of Paul's estate that is more than $50,001, is $14 per $1,000. Some simple ideas such as segregated funds, guaranteed investment funds, guaranteed investment accounts, and GICs through life insurance companies could have saved a lot of time and money. In order to simplify your estate, consider investments with life insurance companies where you can name beneficiaries. Ask your current advisors if they can recommend investments with insurance companies. If they cannot, you may not be looking at all of your available options.

To accumulate wealth, you must study and emulate those who have acquired it before you.
Brian Tracy

Money is better than poverty, if only for financial reasons.
Woody Allen

Mistake 39
NOT HAVING TAX-FREE SAVINGS ACCOUNTS (IF YOU HAVE SAVINGS)

What is better than tax-free? RRSPs were first introduced in 1957 to assist self-employed individuals and employees who were not members of a registered pension plan (RPP) save for their own retirement. Quite simply, a RRSP is an investment plan registered with the Canada Revenue Agency (CRA). Billions have been poured into RRSPs since they were first introduced. Now the next wave is the tax-free savings account (TFSA) or, as I like to call it, tax-free investment account.

Canadian residents 18 years of age or older can open a TFSA if they have filed a tax return. Simply put, you can contribute a maximum of $5,000 per year, and your earnings will be tax-free. It doesn't sound like much in the first year, but each year you can add your personal maximum and over 3, 5, or even 10 years, it adds up, tax-free. You will be able to invest in a variety of options from GICs and savings accounts to mutual funds, and every financial institution in Canada is competing for your TFSA account.

If you take money out of your TFSA, you don't lose the contribution room—you get it back in the following year, but you will have to wait until the next year before you can put the money back in. As with RRSPs, the contribution room gets carried forward each year, and you can hold more than one TFSA account up to an annual maximum of $5,000 per person—that's $10,000 per year for couples.

The big bonuses for retirees are that it will not affect Federal income-tested benefits and credits, so it will be easier to save, and you can name a beneficary, so it passes tax-free to your estate. Why not earn interest, now that it is tax-free, inside a TFSA account? You are also creating a larger tax-free estate. You can use it to name specific beneficiaries if you wish to give cash right away for immediate needs.

Always remember to get professional legal and financial advice when doing estate planning.

Before you can really start setting financial goals, you need to determine where you stand financially.
David Bach

In God we trust, all others pay cash.
American saying

Mistake 40
NOT UNDERSTANDING THE BENEFITS CANADIAN LIFE INSURANCE COMPANY PRODUCTS CAN OFFER IN ESTATE AND RETIREMENT PLANNING

Segregated Fund Benefits

Steve from Parksville dropped by with a question on guaranteed investment funds, also known as segregated funds. Steve wondered why so many retirees look at segregated funds for investing. He brought in a brochure that outlined some of the benefits including guarantee of principal at deposit maturity (in this case 10 years) and 100% upon death; resetting of the guarantee when the market value of the investment fluctuates; and an immediate transfer of funds upon death without probate and/or estate fees. Reading over the brochure more carefully revealed all of the details and options available for Steve; for example, most of his favorite mutual funds are offered as segregated funds. He can put money into a variety of different investments and still have the same manager and style he has now. He was thinking of switching from mutual funds to segregated funds to simplify his estate. While some of his funds are in RRIFs and some are outside his registered plans, the switch could have some tax implications. Inside his RRIF, he can simply transfer from one plan to another just like a RRSP tax-free transfer.

The final question Steve had was that, if the risks are the same because the investments are the same, why do most retirees not take advantage of these options and guarantees. My answer was simple–not everyone has heard of segregated funds.

I wrote an article introducing segregated funds. After receiving calls asking me to discuss them in more detail, I thought I would write out a list of benefits and features. While each investment or insurance company has its own features, segregated funds in general are comprised of a pool of investments, professionally managed by different investment managers and administered by life insurance companies. The life insurance companies add the benefits that can make these investments more attractive than mutual funds. Here is the list:

-100% of your investment guaranteed upon death to your beneficiaries, no loss of capital. Not all plans have this option, so check with your insurance company.

-A maturity guarantee of 100% of your principal investment regardless of market conditions.

-Maturity guarantee reset and death benefit guarantee on a higher amount. (While your investment grows, so does your guarantee upon maturity and to your beneficiaries, thus locking in future profits for you and your family.)

-Creditor protection for professionals and small-business owners. (Under the Insurance Act, you have the potential of protecting those investments from creditors. A professional such as accountant, dentist, doctor, or small-business owner may benefit.)

-Estate planning benefits, such as no probate, no public record of probate, and 100% of the investment passing directly to your beneficiaries instead of through your estate. (I could list a subset of advantages under this benefit.)

-Access to most of the top-performing investment managers available to build a truly diversified and well-managed portfolio.

If you want to add contractual written guarantees to your investments, then segregated funds may be worth a closer look.

GIA, GIC, and Other Acronyms

Every day we are exposed to jargon. In the financial industry, there can be a lot of terms. I have come to an understanding that people want feelings and emotions, not words. People who are retired and concerned about protecting their income, about health and medical costs, about living alone or in a care facility, and/or about running out of money.

In financial terms, they may look at insurance plans such as long-term care, critical-illness or disability insurance.

We (financial professionals) define things in our own language. We define people who want their money to grow as investors looking for growth, higher-risk investors, equity investors, or holders of common stock portfolios. We define retirees seeking a monthly cash flow to live comfortably without losing any capital as income investors. They would invest into segregated funds, GIAs (guaranteed term deposits issued through life insurance companies) GICs, conservative portfolios, income funds, real return bonds, etc. Families worried about protecting income would look at life insurance, disability or income-replacement plans, and group insurance benefits.

Retirees talk about income; the financial industry talks about systematic withdrawal programs, redemption plans, return of capital, dividends, interest, and capital gains income. Investors talk about rate of return and expectations; the financial industry shows statements and numbers and projections, past and future. Ask me what is a back-to-back annuity, and I'll ask you if you want guaranteed income and whether you want to have the same amount paid out to your children when you die.

One term you will need to know is GMWB, discussed on the next few pages.

You want a simple financial plan to get you to where you are going. The financial industry throws you gobs of paper, plans, brochures, projections, and statements. Keep it simple; know what you want; know your financial values (e.g., enough money to spend monthly and extra money annually in your retirement years to live comfortably); then create a plan that you understand and can follow. This will simplify the jargon.

Looking for Guarantees?

We know that in life there are two guarantees, death and taxes. We can go out and buy life insurance to insure ourselves for our loved ones in case of death, and the benefit is tax-free. But how can we invest our money and accomplish the same benefits?

Look into segregated funds. They allow you to name a beneficiary and some plans can guarantee 100% of your investment to your estate upon death regardless of market value. This can give your family added peace of mind in a world of volatility. You can even add on a benefit called GMWB, or guaranteed minimum withdrawal benefit, and guarantee your income for life at a certain age. For example, Edna from Qualicum, who is 65, invested $100,000 into segregated funds and $100,000 into a GIC, naming her two children as beneficiaries–this will bypass probate and simplify her estate. The money is 100% guaranteed upon death regardless of market value, and Edna will receive a minimum of 5% income guaranteed for her lifetime. As an added bonus the income paid to her is not all interest income since the GMWB generates tax-efficient income, making the plan more attractive (and Edna pays less tax).

Now Edna has some guarantees. Upon her death the money is 100% guaranteed to her family for the full amount without probate fees, her income is guaranteed for life at 5%, and she has a guaranteed interest rate on the GIC. Ask your financial professional how you can generate guarantees.

GMWB

In the next few years, every Canadian investor will know this acronym. If you are retiring soon or are already retired, you should know that GMWB stands for guaranteed minimum withdrawal benefit. This will be the largest change in retirement planning I have seen in twenty years.

We know that a GIC can add safety and security in retirement; however, rates change. GMWB plans can offer a predictable income guaranteed not to decrease for life. GMWB plans are offered by Canadian life insurance companies and, as the name suggests, offer guaranteed minimum withdrawal benefits, usually at 5% to 6% (depending on your age at the time) for the rest of your life. The plan gives you sustainable, guaranteed income that is designed to resemble a pension plan. The income has the potential to increase to keep pace with inflation and, unlike pension plans, investors have access to their savings at any time. (However, this can change the guarantees.) The investor can have the potential of market gains and yet has the guaranteed cash flow no matter what the market losses are.

GMWB plans address two unique retirement risks. First, if you are retired and worried about outliving your savings, a properly set up GMWB can guarantee your income for life. Second, you run the risk of depleting your savings or capital due to bad investments, poor investment decisions, or taking on too much risk. A GMWB plan tackles these risks in ways that traditional investments fail—to guarantee investors their future. The GMWB carries a minimal cost compared to risking a lot of money.

The additional benefits of GMWB plans are that they can be set up in nonregistered investment accounts and the income is tax-efficient and guaranteed for life. GMWB plans are only offered through life insurance companies, which means you must name a beneficiary; this means it will bypass probate fees and ensure an easy transition to your estate. Currently there are six Canadian insurance companies offering GMWB plans—all with guarantees for your retirement. Ask your financial advisor today whether GMWB guaranteed plans fit into your retirement.

GMWB versus GIC

Brett from Courtenay dropped by my office and asked me a great question. What is the difference between GMWBs and GICs? Brett, aged 65, recently retired and has his nest egg to invest for retirement income. I first explained that GMWB plans use a wide variety of segregated fund investments inside the plans. Insurance companies can add contractual guarantees like an annuity or pension plan on top of your investments and charge a fee to give you additional guarantees. GICs, however, cannot guarantee income for life or offer a 100% death benefit like some GMWB plans. GMWBs have the added benefit of bypassing probate and simplifying one's estate when a beneficiary is named. GICs guarantee the capital and interest for a specified period of time, usually from one to five years.

"Brett," I said, "if your goal is to plan for a secure retirement with predictable and sustainable income without worrying about the value of your investments, it may be worthwhile to look into GMWBs as part of your overall plan."

GMWBs are flexible and give you access to your savings, but if you need additional income or capital down the road, you usually take that money from other investments since taking it from GMWBs could affect your guarantees.

While GICs are used for accumulating and preserving assets, GMWBs are designed for investors turning their investments into income in retirement and accumulating before retirement.

GICs can pay income monthly (sometimes at a lower rate) for the length of the term. GMWBs pay income guaranteed for life depending on your age.

With GICs you know that the capital stays the same and that your risk is low; with GMWBs the capital can fluctuate and you can choose different levels of risk with the money invested.

While each one has guarantees, your choice depends on what type of guarantee you want. That is the better question. Ask your financial professional about the type of guarantees you are looking for in your investments and retirement.

Don't Leave a Lump Sum of Money

You've worked all your life to save for retirement. Now you've found that you're not going to be able to spend it all; or worse, you are afraid to spend your money. You're saving it for your children. But there is a bigger problem. One child may not be capable of receiving a large lump sum of money if you die due to inability to manage money, his or her personal situation, or mental health issues. Your plan for your child may be to pay out income for five or ten years or for their lifetime. How do you do this?

One alternative is to set up a trust with a named trustee. The trust then pays out to your child in accordance with the trust. This can be very costly and time-consuming. There is an alternative. It is a wealth-transfer option available to Canadians, simple and flexible, called an "annuity settlement."

Here's an example of how it works. Bob and Mary invest $500,000 into a guaranteed investment fund with a life insurance company. They have complete flexibility and control over the money while they are alive. They don't want their son, Sam, to have a lump sum because they are worried about his ability to manage money and prefer to have it paid out over time. After discussing the situation, they select a fifteen-year payout to Sam as the beneficiary. The insurance company will take care of this automatically after they die; it can be paid monthly or annually. It avoids probate fees, legal and executors' fees, sales charges, or estate fees. The insurance company invests it and pays out principal and interest over the fifteen years; it's that simple. It may eliminate the need for a trust and ensures Sam will not receive a lump sum. It can provide parents of disabled children with an estate planning tool, as it allows changing beneficiaries and settlement options quickly and without fees. The plan can ensure children and grandchildren receive income over time rather than in a lump sum. It is a commonly-used tool that can be incorporated into your estate plan if you foresee problems.

Inheritance Planning

Leaving your estate to your intended beneficiaries can take some planning. Here are some strategies to consider.

First, consider spreading out a lump sum payment into a series of payments over time. For example, you can set up a life insurance contract with an annuity settlement option. The payments can be made over five, ten, or fifteen years, as you state in the contract. This way you can leave part of your estate as a lump sum and part of it as regular income.

Second, minimize the impact of probate fees. The fees are one aspect, but the time it takes to settle an estate can be lengthy.

Avoid these two concerns by investing into GICs or segregated funds with life insurance companies. The money is paid out by the life insurance company directly to the person(s) named as beneficiaries. It can work well for second marriages, where each person wants to leave funds to their children without going through the estate. RRSPs and RRIFs can also be set up under a life insurance company; however, most investors name his or her spouse as beneficiary because it is a tax-free transfer to the surviving spouse upon death.

Third, make sure your will is up to date. If you have experienced any major changes in your life, reviewing your will is important in planning. If you have received money from an estate, you know that lack of a will can cause confusion amongst beneficiaries.

Fourth, to prevent any family disputes or concerns, make sure you discuss your estate plan with your family. You can put all the related documents in a binder. Keep it up to date so that there is less confusion and an easier process.

Do what you can, with what you have, where you are.
Theodore Roosevelt

It is not the mountain we conquer, but ourselves.
Sir Edmund Hillary

Mistake 41
NOT UNDERSTANDING PROBATE OR ESTATE PLANNING COSTS

In common usage, probate refers to the process of applying to a court to have a will confirmed as valid and the charge levied by the Court for having done so. Technically the process is an "application for certificate of appointment of estate trustee with a will" and the charge is the "estate administration tax," but in common usage both are still generally called "probate."

Can you legally avoid probate? Yes! There are a number of strategies you can use.

Gift–Property that is given as a gift during your lifetime does not form part of your estate because you do not own it upon your death. The gift becomes the legal property of the recipient. In situations where a testator does not require continued legal control of the asset and where there is no doubt that the recipient is the person who would receive that property upon death, this is the simplest strategy to use.

Joint ownership–Quite often spouses will hold their home in joint ownership with right of survivorship, meaning that the home passes to the surviving spouse. Similar arrangements can be made with individuals other than a spouse, and the type of property need not be restricted to real estate. In fact, many financial assets such as bank accounts and other investments such as term deposits are held jointly with the intention that the account goes to the survivor (or survivors).

Insurance beneficiary designation–Under a life insurance policy you can name a beneficiary who is to receive the death benefit proceeds directly, without the payment passing through the estate. In addition to avoiding probate, any creditors of your estate will be bypassed. This also applies to GICs, term deposits, and segregated funds invested with a life insurance company.

RRSP/RRIF beneficiary designation—As with insurance designations, probate may be avoided for named beneficiaries under RRSPs, RRIFs, and other similarly registered investment plans, although protection against estate creditors may not be available.

More Income, Less Tax, No Probate Fees

How come some retirees have more income and less tax? Let's look at Betty, a 75-year-old retiree in Qualicum Beach. She inherited $200,000 and was looking for income and less tax. She also didn't want to take a lot of risk. While she wanted income she thought she would want access to some capital but not all. We decided to invest half into GICs and half into an annuity. Here is what Betty ended up with.

The annuity for $100,000 provided her with $774 per month guaranteed as long as she lives. That's $9,288 per year that will always be there for her. We also put in a guarantee to her children for ten years' worth of payments. That means the payments will continue until ten years after her death. The second portion was invested into a one-year and a five-year GIC. The average return on those funds is 4% combined. We used the barbell technique, half short-term and half long-term. Because we don't know how interest rates may fluctuate, we take the average, which in this case is 4% (3.4% for the one-year GIS and year and 4.6% for the five-year GIC). Betty's payout will be $4,000 from the GICs. This gives her a combined income of $13,288 per year on $200,000, or approximately 6.64%.

Now comes the tax. Since the GICs are fully taxable, she has $4,000 of interest income. (We invested the GICs with insurance companies so that we could name a beneficiary on the plan—when Betty dies, there is no probate cost.) The taxable portion on the annuity is only $2,494 per year, since we used a prescribed annuity for tax efficiency. Although Betty receives income of $13,288 per year she has taxable income of only $6,494 per year.

Now Betty doesn't have to worry about market risk or a higher tax bill. She has a steady income and less tax. When Betty dies, all of the funds and/or income will go directly to her beneficiaries, free of any probate fees.

The sources of deflation are not a mystery. Deflation is in almost all cases a side effect of a collapse of aggregate demand...a drop in spending so severe that producers must cut prices on an ongoing basis in order to find buyers.
Ben Bernanke

If you can count your money, you don't have a billion dollars.
J. Paul Getty

Mistake 42
FOR SENIORS IN POOR HEALTH, NOT CONSIDERING AN IMPAIRED ANNUITY

There's a type of annuity that pays you more if your health profile is not good. This may sound strange, but here's how it works: SPIA, which stands for single premium immediate annuity, has long been a popular investment for obtaining a fixed income that cannot be outlived. With the lifetime payments option, a SPIA pays you a fixed monthly income for life. Insurance companies calculate the size of your monthly payment based on standard life expectancy tables. Once calculated at the beginning, you continue to receive the same monthly amount, regardless of how long you live. Some companies take into account your individual health condition and use that information to calculate your life expectancy. If your health records indicate conditions that could lower your life expectancy, this is factored into the monthly payment you receive and increases the monthly payment. You then receive this fixed monthly amount no matter how long you live.

Take this hypothetical example: A 70-year-old decides to obtain a SPIA. He deposits a $100,000 premium and, based on his standard life expectancy of sixteen years, his monthly payment is $729 (average payment based on current rates, subject to change). He will receive this fixed monthly amount regardless of how long he lives. However, if he has a negative health profile and the insurance companies calculate his life expectancy to be only ten years, his monthly payment will jump to $1,064.

SPIAs have been most popular with single individuals who are not concerned about leaving an inheritance. That's because once the initial premium is paid, the SPIA cannot be surrendered for value; rather, one receives a fixed monthly income for life.

If you like the idea of increasing your monthly income and you want to leave funds to heirs, you would use only a part of your assets for a SPIA and designate another part for heirs. If you have a poor health history, you may be entitled to more income.

If you want to say it with flowers, a single rose says, 'I'm cheap!'
Delta Burke

*Every day I get up and look through the Forbes list of the richest people in
America. If I'm not there, I go to work.*
Robert Orben

Mistake 43
LEAVING YOUR SPOUSE BROKE

Have you established a plan to ensure your spouse will continue
to have sufficient income? Many seniors fear the loss of income
when one spouse dies. This is especially true with second
marriages. If the accounts are not held jointly, they may be left
to the other spouse's children, leaving you with little or no
resources. Making sure all assets, including vehicles, are jointly
registered assures the assets will be transferred with no probate
and without passing through the will. Will having assets invested
separately place a financial hardship on your surviving spouse?

Assets registered in joint names do not trigger taxation; rather,
a simple re-registration; but if assets are invested in individual
names, the asset is considered to be sold on the date of death and
(unnecessary) taxes must be paid, possibly leaving your spouse
with less money. Capital gains can reduce the value of the asset
and reduce your spouse's income for his or her lifetime. If the
asset is registered in your name only, check whether there is any
tax payable to re-register the asset.

Your will probably states that the assets are to transfer to your
surviving spouse. But if this is your second marriage or if there
are large capital gains on the assets, this may not happen in the
manner you think. It's not that simple when assets pass through
the will. Also, any fees, charges, executor fees, delays, and taxes
can be avoided by jointly registering assets. There can be similar
challenges in a common-law relationship.

The best thing you can do right now is to review how your assets
are owned, who is named as your beneficiary, and the language
of your estate planning documents. Then check with your legal

advisor and financial institution or financial advisor; these people are knowledgeable about estate planning and can help to guide you and your spouse.

It isn't necessary to be rich and famous to be happy. It's only necessary to be rich.
Alan Alda

A bank is a place where they lend you an umbrella in fair weather and ask for it back when it rains.
Robert Frost

Mistake 44
NO CONSIDERATION FOR LONG-TERM HEALTH AND ELDER CARE

The next big wave in retirement planning is elder care and elder care insurance. The number of clients worrying about their estate pales in comparison to the number of people worrying about elder care and health problems. Who is going to look after your finances if you go into a seniors' home or hospital or if you get Alzheimer's? It is a growing problem as the population in Canada ages.

Let me give you an example of a couple with whom I recently spoke. She has the beginning phases of dementia and realizes that she won't be able to look after her finances. Her assets are registered in her name, because this is a second marriage. She needs to update her will and power of attorney; however, if her lawyer deems her incapable she will be stuck with an outdated will and power of attorney. We discovered also that the beneficiaries of her RRSPs and life insurance are her two children, since she made the designation before she got married. If she can no longer make financial decisions, she cannot change her beneficiary; and her husband will have to take financial care of her without any inheritance when she passes away. A challenging case. A few simple but important steps can help this situation.

There is a challenge in that her previous financial planner was helping to get everything out of the estate to save probate fees, and the lawyer wanted everything in the estate because of the second marriage. First, if you want assets out of the estate, naming beneficiaries is key. Second, put assets in joint names with your beneficiaries. You can have more than one name on an investment; for example, an investor who holds a term deposit can make it jointly owned with a child (or children) or spouse. Third, make sure your will is up to date along with a power of attorney.

If you're concerned about elder care, this should be discussed with whoever holds your power of attorney. This person should be able to act on your behalf when the time comes. If you do not have people that can act on your behalf, find someone who can. Recently, I have discussed with local accountants and lawyers their ability to act to help clients in similar situations.

Finally, discuss your concerns with your family and spell out what you would like done. It can take a lot of stress off a family knowing things are planned out. Check out the new elder care insurance policies to protect yourself and your estate. While exploring insurance options, ask your insurance professional about long-term care insurance and critical illness insurance to see which is right for you.

I don't like money, actually, but it quiets my nerves.
Joe Louis

More and more these days I find myself pondering how to reconcile my net income with my gross habits.
John Nelson

Mistake 45
NOT HAVING AN ESTATE PLANNING TEAM

Paying out an estate can sometimes be as complicated as preparing for an estate. When we hear from an executor that a client has passed away, it's critical for us to put together an estate planning team. The executor may have a big job ahead of him or her. First, we need to hear from the executor(s). Second, we usually require a notarized copy of the will and of the death certificate; and the solicitor for the estate helps gather the relevant documents. Third, the tax returns have to be prepared; and before large lump sums of money can be paid out, the taxes have to be calculated and returns filed. Fourth, claims on all life insurance policies need to be completed. If trusts are involved, we will need instructions on investing, managing, or distributing trust funds.

To help your executor(s) complete the estate from start to finish, you can assemble your own team. This would include:

-A legal advisor who will review your estate and draft wills and trusts. He or she can also administrate and represent your estate.

-A financial advisor who will help develop estate planning goals, cooperate and work with other professionals on your team, review and update your plans, provide ideas to help make the most of your estate, and gather all the documents into an estate plan.

-A tax professional who will assist in planning to reduce or minimize your estate tax liability and suggest or implement any tax strategies and/or income splitting with a spouse.

Finding a team and discussing the team with your executor can be a great step towards the best estate plan for you and, more importantly, your spouse and family.

Your Estate Plan

An estate plan prepares your spouse and family and provides peace of mind for you. Here are four tips on preparing an estate plan.

1. Draw up a will. Name an appropriate executor and guardians for any minor children and make financial provisions for your spouse and family.

2. Establish power of attorney. Down the road you may not be able to make financial or medical decisions for yourself. A power of attorney is a legal document arranging for someone to make those decisions while you are alive. It differs from a will since it is only active while you are alive.

3. Use life insurance. Life insurance can provide some significant benefits to a spouse and family, including replacing your income upon death and paying estate costs such as taxes, debts, and funeral expenses. Whether you have enough depends on the needs of your beneficiaries. Do you want to provide for your loved ones and keep them in the same lifestyle? How much income would they require and for how long?

4. Put assets outside your estate. While a will designates who receives your estate, it is costly in probate fees, administration expenses, and time. Investing with life insurance companies bypasses your estate and can include segregated funds (similar to mutual funds), GICs, term deposits, and annuities. Normally you don't name beneficiaries on mutual funds or term deposits; but if you invest through a life insurance company, each investment has a beneficiary and carries the advantages of no probate fees, no delays, and not being a matter of public record. Estates that are probates go through the Court, which is a matter of public record, but your beneficiaries receive the funds directly from the life insurance company.

Estate planning is unique in that every family is unique and has different needs. Having a written estate plan (suggestion–keep it in a binder) and sharing it with your spouse and family is a valuable way of preparing for your spouse and family.

Estate Planning and Joint Last-to-die Insurance

The goal of an estate plan is to have more of your money available to you and your survivors, and less available to the Government and outsiders. Many estate plans include the use of joint last-to-die life insurance. This type of insurance generally covers two people under the same policy; the death benefit is paid when the second person dies. Such coverage is desirable in situations where the individuals share a common liability, such as taxation of a RRSP, RRIF, or capital gains.

Many estate planning strategies defer the payment of tax for as long as possible; for example, upon death a taxpayer is deemed to have disposed of all capital property at fair market value. If the property has increased in value from when it was acquired, the increase is a capital gain subject to taxation. Joint last-to-die insurance is the perfect solution for funding this tax liability, because the funds become available exactly when they are needed–upon the second death.

In the Canadian insurance marketplace, there are significant differences in the costs of joint last-to-die insurance. In determining the cost of this coverage, life insurance companies generally convert, by way of an actuarial calculation, the ages of the two lives insured into an equivalent single life age (commonly referred to as the "ESLA"). The price of the policy is then based on the ESLA.

The use of life insurance as part of an estate plan is very common, but it is important to understand that life insurance must be structured properly to ensure funds are available when they are needed. Therefore, it is important to ensure that joint last-to-die insurance is only used in situations where the liability or need for cash arises upon the death of the last person insured.

The only reason I made a commercial for American Express was to pay for my American Express bill.
Peter Ustinov

If there is anyone to whom I owe money, I'm prepared to forget it if they are.
Errol Flynn

Mistake 46
CAN A RRIF REALLY BE GUARANTEED FOR LIFE?

Some companies claim that a RRIF can be guaranteed for life. I understand that an annuity is guaranteed for life, but how can you guarantee a RRIF for life? Some life insurance companies provide for retirees age 65 and over a guaranteed stream of income, regardless of investment performance for their lifetime. When you are 65 or older and looking at taking risk with your RRSP or RRIF, it would be nice to have some guarantees.

Looking closely at several different insurance company plans, I discovered some unique features for retirees. These include a guaranteed 5% income floor throughout retirement, even if the market value of the RRIF investment reduces to zero. Another guarantee is that in years no RRIF income is taken (i.e., no RRIF minimum is required to be paid in the first year), a 5% bonus increases the guaranteed annual income, giving retirement income an initial boost. Some companies also allow you to automatically reset your RRIF every three years; and that allows you to lock in investment gains when markets rise and increase future annual guaranteed income, for life. If you set up your plan options a certain way, you may also have the flexibility to withdraw more than the guaranteed income amount to meet the required RRIF minimum without affecting future guaranteed stream of lifetime payments.

When looking at income options from your RRIF in the future, wouldn't it be nice to have an income guarantee of 5% for the rest of your life, regardless of market value? That is why a lot of retirees look to GICs for their RRIF–because of the guarantees. Now you have another option, guaranteed minimum withdrawal plans that work like an annuity and are offered by Canadian life insurance companies.

The safe way to double your money is to fold it over once and put it in your pocket.
Frank Hubbard

A bank is a place that will lend you money if you can prove that you don't need it.
Bob Hope

Mistake 47
NOT UNDERSTANDING MONEY

One of the most important things a financial advisor has to remember is that most people don't understand money; they understand what money does for them! For example; do you like working on your automobile? Do you really want to know how the transmission works and how it is connected with all the other components in your engine, and how they are all interrelated? I don't either. We have more important things to worry about–having a reliable car and, of course, a trustworthy mechanic to fix it.

Money is the same. People understand how to spend money; they just don't understand how all of the financial details interrelate with each other. Think about it. When the issues of retirement planning, income taxes, estate planning, investments, and insurance are combined, who can understand all of it? In fact, how many of you ever find yourselves confused about the income tax laws? Many people do not understand what percentages mean. Thus it is imperative to take these complicated financial matters and translate then into easy-to-understand concepts.

Most investors want the bottom line–how the investment is going to help achieve life goals, such as:

-Keeping better pace with inflation in retirement.

-Having more spendable income in retirement.

-Reducing income taxes to have more cash flow to enjoy.

-Reducing estate taxes for peace of mind.

-Affording more vacations.

-Helping children and grandchildren.

-Maintaining a comfortable lifestyle on one's own terms.

When dealing with your money it is imperative to incorporate the benefits into your investments. I had a friend tell me, "I don't know what the money will be used for." Once you clearly know what the money is for, you will have a lot less worry about it.

The Magic of Wealth

The word "wealthy" means different things to different people. You might think it means lots of money, riches, real estate, and cash. As a retirement planning specialist, dealing with money and seeing financially successful people on a daily basis, to me "wealthy" means the right combination of time and money. You see, we measure wealth by a bank account or net worth, but we all have the same amount of time in a day. We are on equal footing. You don't have ten more minutes in your day than I do, yet how you choose to spend your time may be very different. We all choose how we spend or save money. We do the same thing with our time. It is very precious and we see how precious it can be when thousands die in a natural disaster.

But how much time do you want? Some people never retire because they don't know how to spend their time. They know how to spend their money, but time is a challenge. Do you spend your time wisely? Does it seem that you never have enough hours in the day? Could you spend your time better?

I have seen a lot of wealthy people who do not enjoy their money. I've seen a lot of less-fortunate people really enjoy their family time. Here's a secret: Time is not money, it is way more valuable. Finding the right amount of time and money is the key to wealth. When you find it, let me know; I've been looking for years...

Don't marry for money. You can borrow it cheaper.
Scottish Proverb

I have enough money to last me the rest of my life, unless I buy something.
Jackie Mason

Mistake 48
NOT UNDERSTANDING WHAT
PROFESSIONAL HELP CAN DO

I held a meeting with several clients and asked them what question would be most interesting to the public. The answer amazed me. The number one question was: What is a financial planner (advisor) and what does he or she do? If you ask any of my colleagues, you will receive a passionate answer about a career they find very rewarding.

A financial advisor is someone who will listen to your unique situation, ask you questions to help you on the road to financial discovery, and build a road map to help you get there. Think of the last big trip you took. You needed to do some planning, find out costs, and look at possible risks. You embarked on the journey to discover, to expand your horizons, and to fulfill some life-long dreams and goals. Now, plan your finances the same way. The help of a financial advisor will provide you with the following benefits: goal-setting, personal attention, education, and guidance through the investing options and jargon. Your advisor is someone with an understanding of your goals. He or she can point out investment opportunities and can help develop tax, estate, banking, and insurance strategies. It works both ways—over time, the more information you provide to your advisor, the more he or she can help you. Discussing expectations at the outset is important, so both parties know what type of financial road map you are going to develop.

A few questions to ask are: How do you get paid? What type of services do you provide? What type of people are your typical clients? What is your background and what are your designations?

So where do you find a financial advisor and how do you choose one? Asking a friend or relative for a referral is common, as well as looking in the yellow pages for banks, insurance companies,

and independent mutual fund dealers. Come prepared–
investment statements, tax returns, insurance policies, and
related documents are usually required to develop your road map
for financial success.

*It's good to have money and the things that money can buy, but
it's good, too, to check up once in a while and make sure that you
haven't lost the things that money can't buy.*
George Horace Lorimer

Chapter 5

ADDITIONAL RESOURCES

MASTERING YOUR RETIREMENT
INCOME PLAN

GRANT HICKS

TAKE ACTION TODAY–RETIREMENT INCOME
PLAN WORKSHEET

1. Go to the Web site <www.ghicks.com/worksheet> and print off the retirement mistakes worksheet and data worksheet.

2. Complete the full questionnaire.

3. Discuss areas of concern with family, if applicable.

4. Call your professional(s)–financial, taxation, and legal; and make an appointment to discuss your areas of concern.

5. Get a second opinion (if necessary) on your finances. Ask friends who are the same age and who have similar risk tolerances who they would recommend.

6. Make sure you have a written plan to follow, and follow your plan. Meet on a regular basis with your financial professional.

7. If it is the same plan you had three to five years ago, you are due for an update or second opinion. Call your financial professional or seek a second opinion.

AFTERWORD

Reward yourself. It's great to set goals and plans, but along the way as you improve and find the things you enjoy most, plan to have a rewarding retirement during which you can do the things you love.

IMPORTANT DISCLAIMER PLEASE READ

This is not a recommendation for sale of any product or service. Always consult with your financial professional, accountant, tax professional, legal professional, lawyer, and team of professional financial advisors before proceeding on any idea contained in this book. It is up to you to get professional advice before making any decisions. This is a summary of articles written by Grant Hicks and does not constitute any advice given to anyone in any financial situation. Remember, always consult with your financial professional.

BOOK SUMMARY

While I have been putting together some common retirement planning mistakes I have seen in the past twenty years, I have had great conversations with great retired investors. Their plans are based on logical decisions and not on opinions. The great investors don't do it themselves, because they know it is an emotional decision. They come to the logical conclusion that they need a team of great professionals to help avoid retirement mistakes and to become comfortable with their retirement plans. And in order to be comfortable with their retirement plans, they need to have a written framework, plan, or foundation. Just like a flight plan.

Years ago at a retirement planning conference, I heard of a great analogy for retirement planning. I am the Captain of a large airplane heading to Hawaii. I have a timetable and a flight plan. I have a schedule and a manifest. However, along the way, we may run into airport, mechanical, or maintenance problems or weather delays. Once we are flying there may be turbulence and more weather problems. Upon arrival there could also be problems and delays.

However, I remember two things. First, I did not build the airplane, it is mechanical and sometimes things break down and need repairing. It can be fixed. Second, I do not control the weather or the airport. Weather changes constantly and airports can be very stressful as schedules constantly change due to weather or other factors. However, at the end of the day I will get you to your destination—as your Captain, that is my job and as long as you don't plan to jump out at 30,000 feet, I will get you there.

That is the job of a financial professional, financial planner or advisor, or retirement specialist—to help you create a flight plan and to help you get to your destination.

ABOUT THE AUTHOR

Grant Hicks, RDB, CIM, FCSI, is a professional speaker, writer,

co-author and a Retirement Planning Specialist with Hicks Financial on Vancouver Island, British Columbia. Since starting Hicks Financial in 1989, Grant has developed a specialty in working with retirees and those about to retire using his retirement process, *The Island Lifestyle Retirement Planning Program*©. Grant helps people avoid common mistakes made in retirement and shares more than twenty years of experience helping people avoid them in his book *Canadian Retirement Planning Mistakes, Key Strategies on How to Take Action to Avoid Them,* published by Trafford.

Grant is a Registered Deposit Broker (RDB) and has earned the

Canadian Investment Manager (CIM) portfolio management designation from the Canadian Securities Institute. Grant is also a Fellow of the Canadian Securities Institute–the highest mark of professionalism in the Canadian Securities Industry. Representing individual integrity and unrivalled professionalism, the designation of Fellow of CSI (FCSI)® is reserved for financial services professionals who have met the most exacting standards for industry experience, advanced education, and solid endorsement from their peers and superiors.

Grant is a well known financial authority among retirees. He teaches retirement courses at Vancouver Island University Elder College. He writes a regular column on retirement planning in the *PQB News* and on <www.myseniorsite.ca>, a retirement planning Web site based on Vancouver island.

Married with two children and a golden lab, Grant played professional hockey in Europe before starting Hicks Financial in 1989. Grant lives in beautiful Parksville, British Columbia, on Vancouver Island.

TESTIMONIALS

A top pension fund manager in Canada once told me that everybody is too focused on market value while pension funds are all about 'going concern' value. Retirement is about ongoing living, not cashing out. Grant's book simplifies the concepts in a way that the average person can understand. He strips away the mystique and shares his wisdom and insight in a straightforward way. This should be required reading for everybody over 50.
Jim Graddon, Oakville, Ontario

At a young age, Grant has really figured it out. Working with retirees in his business has given him some great insights on what works and doesn't work for retirees. This book has a lot of great financial points for anyone planning to retire. Well done!
Jim Yih, Financial expert, author, and speaker

AUTHOR CONTACT

AND WORKSHOP INFORMATION

The Island Lifestyle Retirement Planning Program© for retirees on Vancouver Island BC. Contact Grant Hicks at 1-866-954-0247 (in BC) or 250-954-0247 and ask for a FREE *Island Lifestyle Retirement* second opinion—a FREE, no-obligation, one-hour consultation.

If you would like to learn more about your retirement, go to <www.ghicks.com> or contact:

Grant Hicks, RDB,CIM,FCSI
PO Box 1950
172 Weld Street
Parksville, BC, V9P 2H7
grant@ghicks.com

Grant is available for speaking engagements and workshops. Grant has been an invited to speak to many organizations including Manulife Financial, AIC Group of Funds, Standard Life, Vancouver Island University, Advocis, RDBA, RBC Dominion Securities, Scotiamcleod, and TD Bank.

Our workshops can accommodate all needs. We can provide anything from a one-hour presentation to a two-day workshop.

BIBLIOGRAPHY

Alexander, Michael. *How to Inherit Money: A Guide to Making Good Financial Decisions After Losing Someone You Love.* Career Press, 1998. Print.

Brinson, Gary P., Brian D. Singer, and Gilbert P. Beebower. "Determinants of Portfolio Performance II." *Financial Analysts Journal,* May/June 1991. Print.

Canada Revenue Agency. Web. <www.cra-arc.gc.ca>.

"Canadian life insurance compensation." Assuris. Web. <http://www.assuris.ca/>.

CDIC Canadian Deposit insurance Corporation. Web. <http://cdic.ca/>.

FICOM Financial Institutions Commission of BC. Web. <www.fic.gov.bc.ca>.

"Government of Canada Web Site for Income Security Programs." Government of Canada. Web. <www.hrsdc.gc.ca>.

Graham, Benjamin. *The Intelligent Investor: The Definitive Book on Value Investing. A Book of Practical Counsel.* Harper Business Essentials, 1973. Print.

Herscu, Larry. *The Canadian Guide to Managed Accounts.* WRAP Publications, 2004. Print.

Matthews, Keith. *The Empowered Investor.* Book Coach, 2008. Print.

Miller, Bill, Robert G. Hagstrom, and Ken Fisher. *The Warren Buffett Way.* Wiley, 2005. Print.

O'Shaughnessy, James. *How to Retire Rich.* Broadway Publishing, 1997. Print.

Prince, Russ Alan. *Wealth Management: The New Business Model for Financial Advisors.* Wealth Management Press, 2003. Print.

RDBA, The Registered Deposit Brokers Association. Web. <http://rdba.ca/>.

INDEX

H

hassle assets 2
health care 105

I

income 111-120
income needs 46, 63, 84
income splitting 72, 96, 127
Income Tax Act 56, 66, 68, 86
inflation 6, 10-11, 45, 48, 55, 62, 69, 71, 75, 78, 81, 114, 132
inheritances 106, 116, 121, 125
insurance 6, 26, 29-30, 35, 37-39, 83-84, 86-87, 92, 95, 97, 100, 105, 107,
    110- 135
insured annuity 30
investment policy statement (IPS) 8, 53
investment portfolio 27, 83
IPS 8, 53

J

joint last-to-die insurance 129
joint life annuity 85
joint ownership with right of survivorship 118

L

last-to-die insurance 129
leverage 86
LIF 38, 73
life annuity 84-85
life income funds (LIF) 38, 73
life insurance 6, 26, 29-30, 35, 37-39, 83-84, 86,-87, 92, 95, 97, 100, 105, 107,
    110-135
locked-in retirement accounts (LIRA, LIF, LRIF) 73
locked-in RRSPs 73, 74, 80
long-term care 112, 126
long-term investments 45, 53
LRIF 73-74

M

managed account 32
managed asset program 19, 27
management fee 53
market risk 10, 120